# TOP 50

MW00812903

**Arranged by Carol Tornquist**

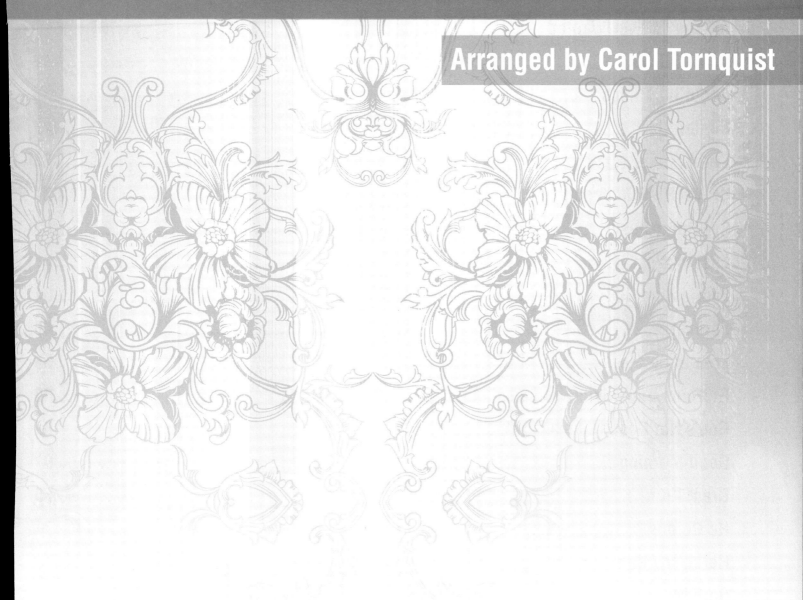

Produced by
Alfred Music
P.O. Box 10003
Van Nuys, CA 91410-0003
**alfred.com**

Printed in USA.

ISBN-10: 1-4706-1027-2
ISBN-13: 978-1-4706-1027-2

Cover art:
Concert crowd: © iStockphoto.com / n0n4m3h3r0 • Yellow-blue background: © Shutterstock.com / wongwean

# TABLE OF CONTENTS

# ALL THE PEOPLE SAID AMEN

Words and Music by Matt Maher,
Paul Moak and Trevor Morgan
Arranged by Carol Tornquist

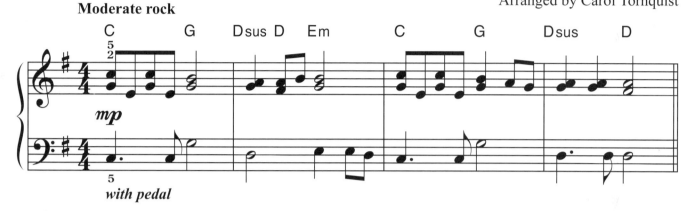

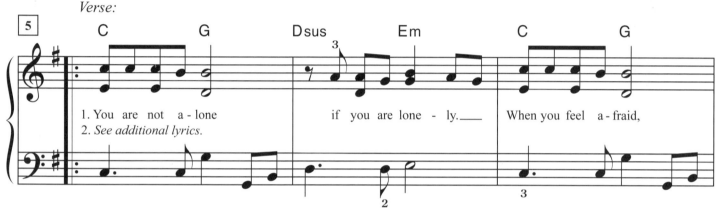

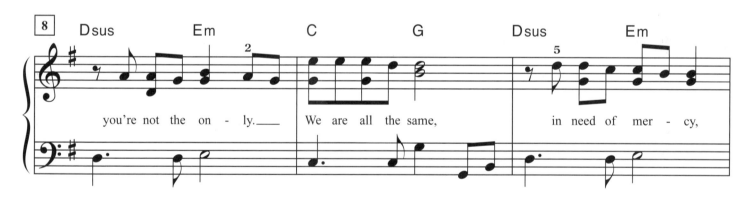

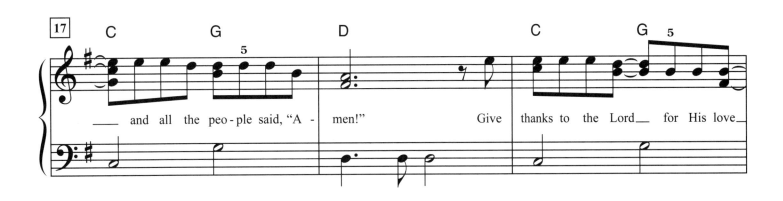

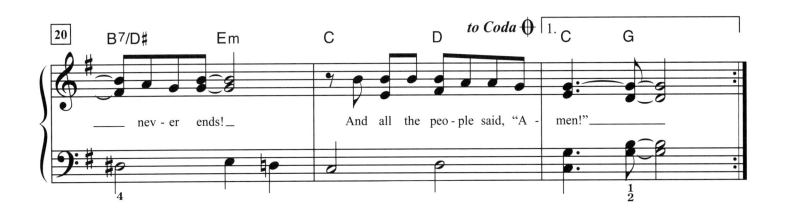

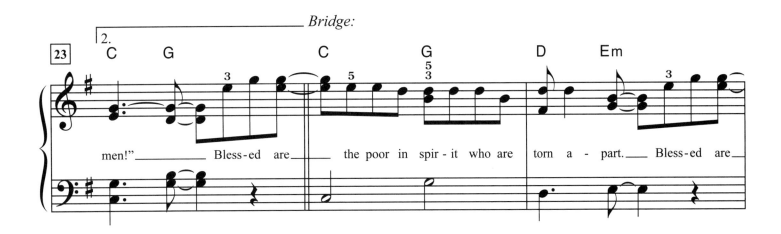

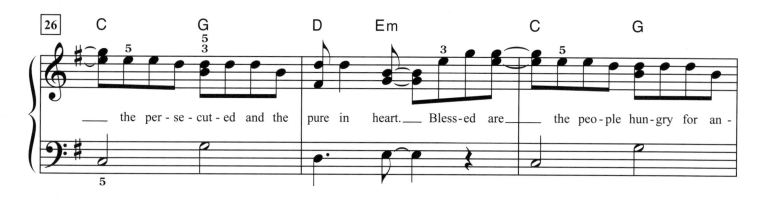

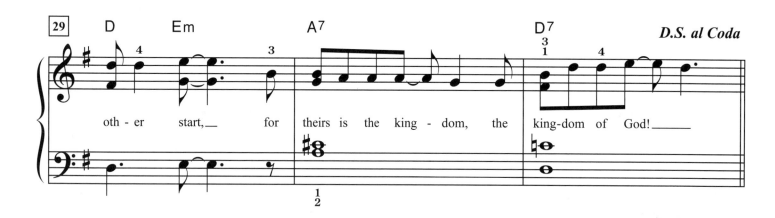

*Verse 2:*
If you're rich or poor, well, it don't matter.
Weak or strong, you know, love is what we're after.
We're all broken, but we're all in this together.
God knows we stumble and fall, and He so loved the world,
He sent His Son to save us all.
*(To Chorus:)*

# ALL YOU'VE EVER WANTED

Words and Music by
Bernie Herms and Mark Hall
Arranged by Carol Tornquist

*Verse 3:*
I was chasing healing when I'd been made well,
I was fighting battles when You conquered hell.
Living free but from a prison cell;
Lord, I lay it down today.

So I'll stop living off of how I feel,
And start standing on Your truth revealed.
Jesus is my strength, my shield,
And He will never fail me.

# BEAUTIFUL DAY

Words and Music by Chris Stevens, Jamie Grace,
Morgan Harper Nichols and Toby McKeehan
Arranged by Carol Tornquist

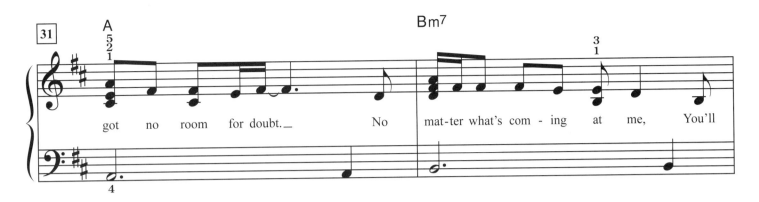

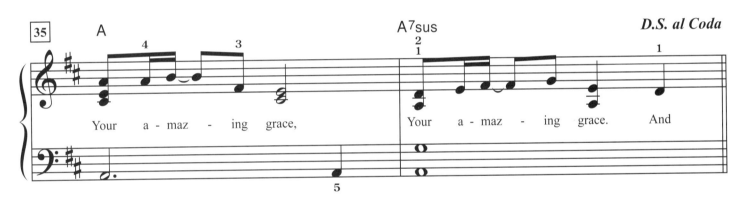

*Verse 2:*
When trouble seems to rain on my dreams, it's not a big, not a big deal.
Let it wash all the bugs off my windshield, 'cause You're showing me in You, I'm free.
And You're still the refuge that I've just gotta get to.
So, I won't let a day go, won't let a day go by.
So put the drop top down, turn it up, I'm ready to fly.
*(To Chorus:)*

# BEAUTIFUL THINGS

Words and Music by
Lisa Gungor and Michael Gungor
Arranged by Carol Tornquist

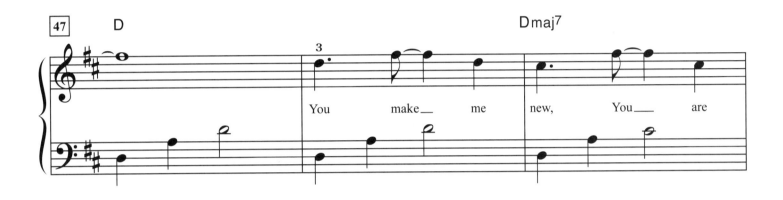

You make____ me new, You____ are

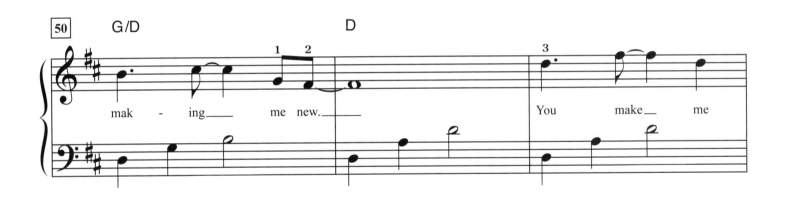

mak - ing____ me new.____ You make____ me

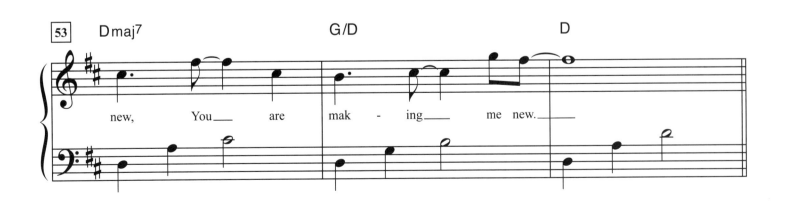

new, You____ are mak - ing____ me new.____

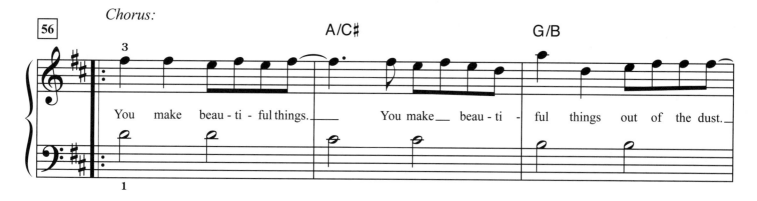

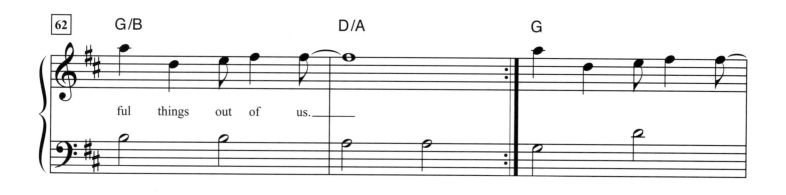

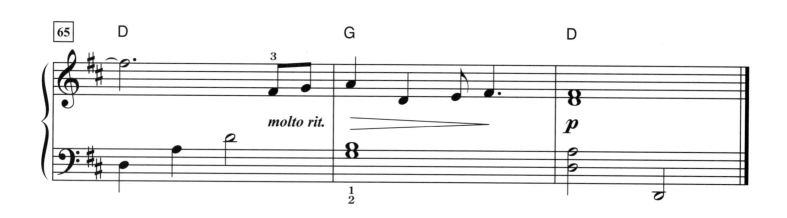

# CINDERELLA

Words and Music by
Steven Curtis Chapman
Arranged by Carol Tornquist

**Gently, in one**

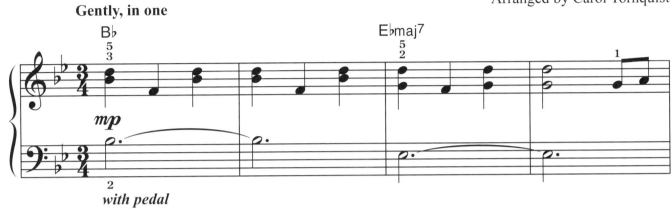

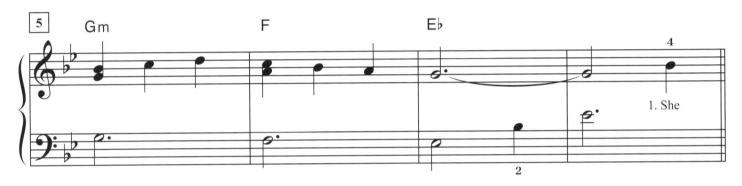

*Verse:*

spins    and    she sways____    to what-ev-er    song
2., 3. *See additional lyrics.*

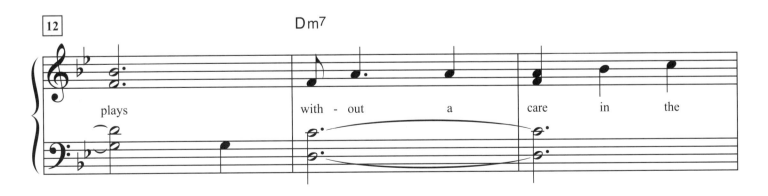

plays    with-out    a    care    in the

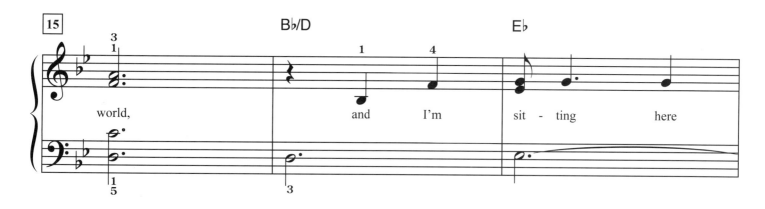

world, and I'm sit - ting here

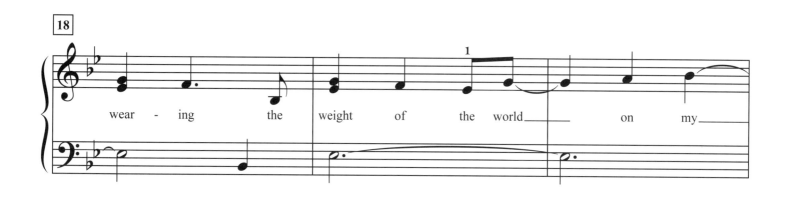

wear - ing the weight of the world on my

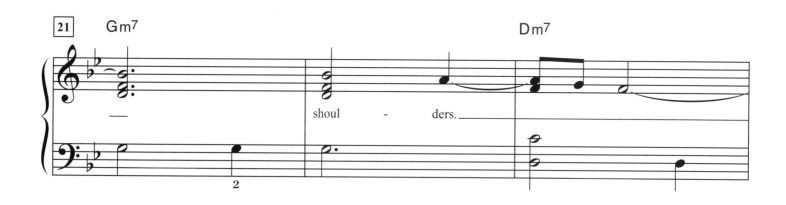

shoul - ders.

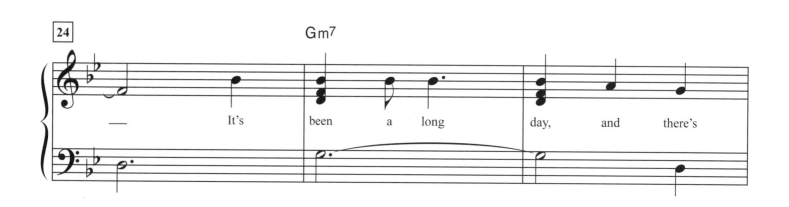

It's been a long day, and there's

Dad - dy, please!" So

*Chorus:*

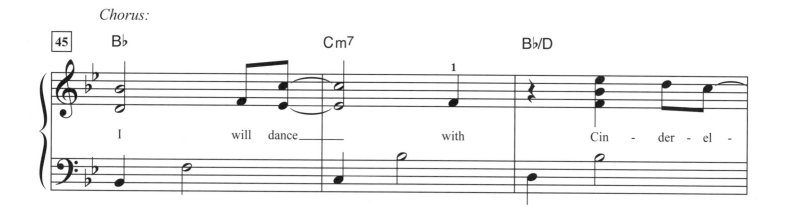

I will dance with Cin - der - el -

la while she is here in my arms,

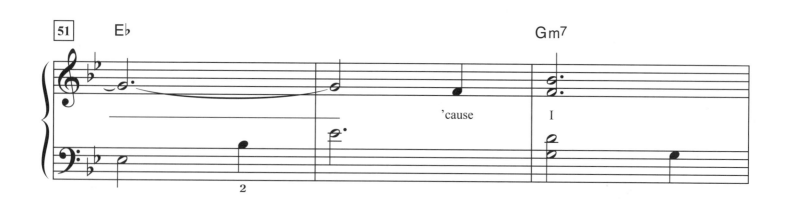

'cause I

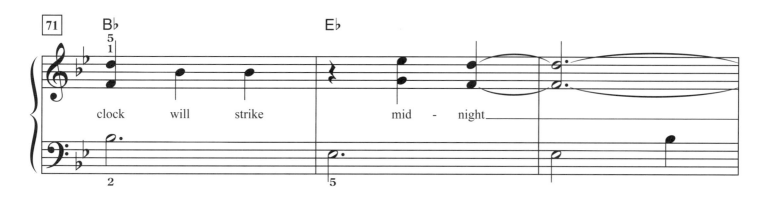

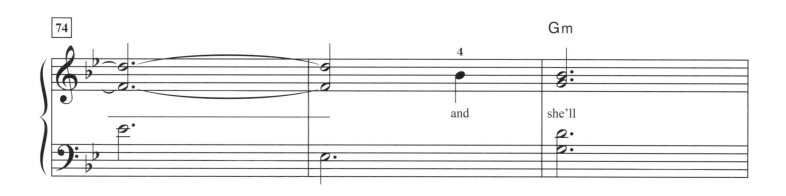

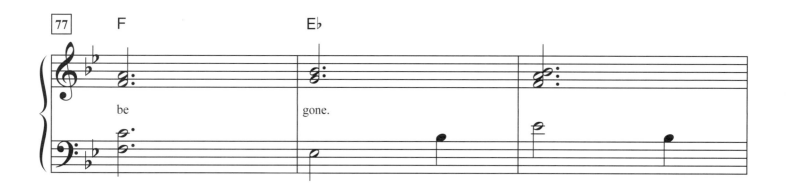

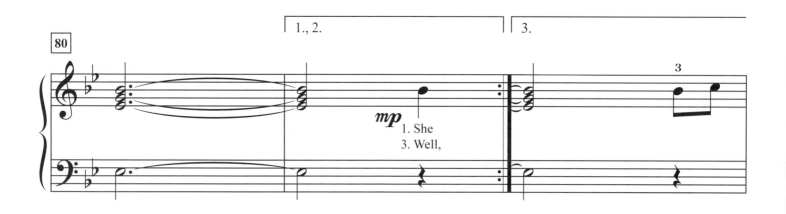

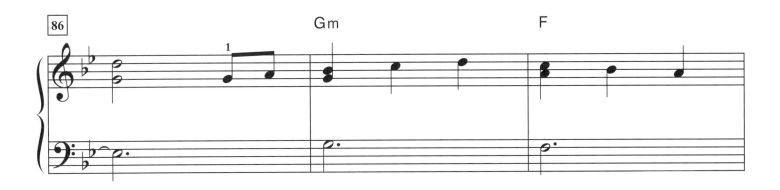

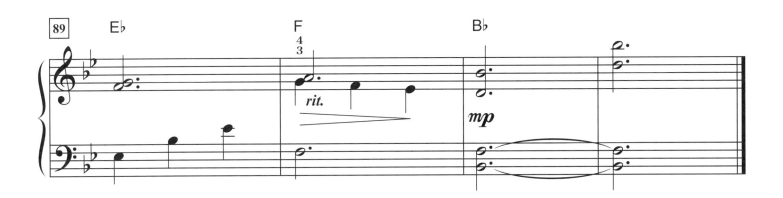

*Verse 2:*
She says he's a nice guy and I'd be impressed;
She wants to know if I approve of her dress.
She says, "Dad, the prom is just one week away,
And I need to practice my dancing.
Oh, please, Daddy, please!"
*(To Chorus:)*

*Verse 3:*
Well, she came home today with a ring on her hand,
Just glowing, and telling all they had planned.
She says, "Dad, the wedding's still six months away,
but I need to practice my dancing.
Oh, please, Daddy, please!"
*(To Chorus:)*

# CORNERSTONE

Words and Music by Edward Mote,
Eric Liljero, Jonas Myrin and Reuben Morgan
Arranged by Carol Tornquist

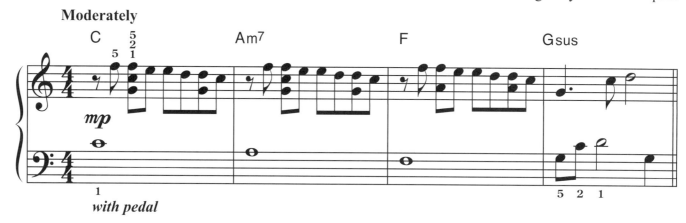

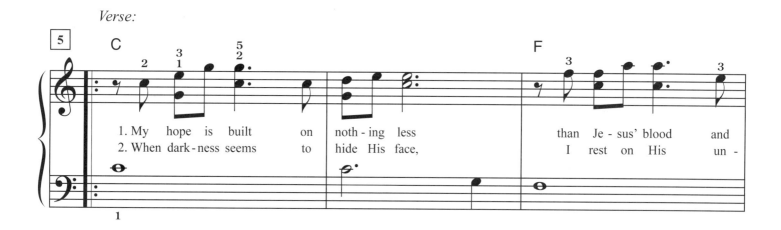

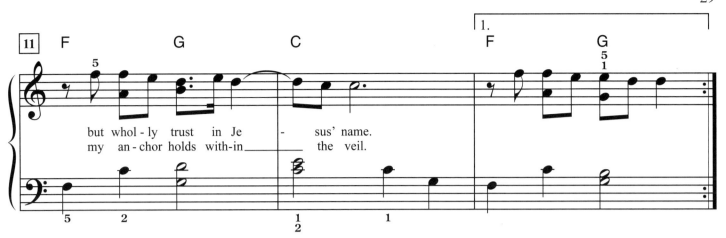

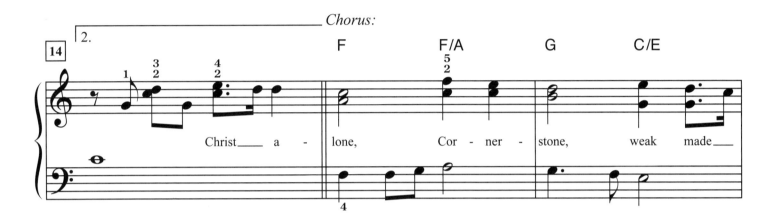

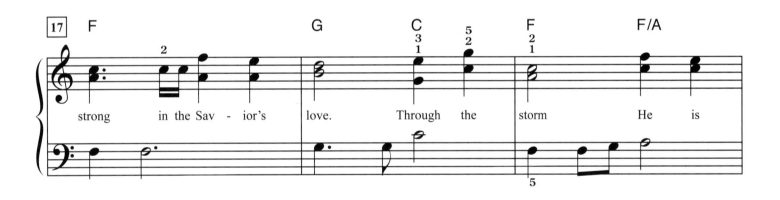

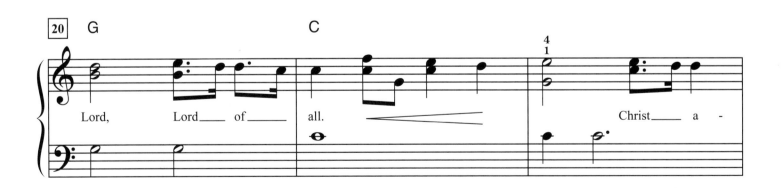

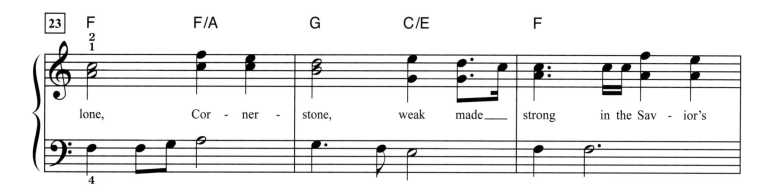

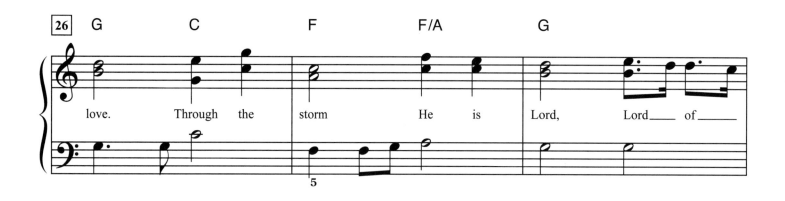

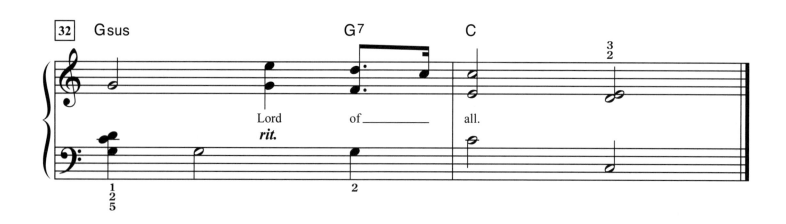

# EVERLASTING GOD

Words and Music by
Brenton Brown and Ken Riley
Arranged by Carol Tornquist

**Brightly**

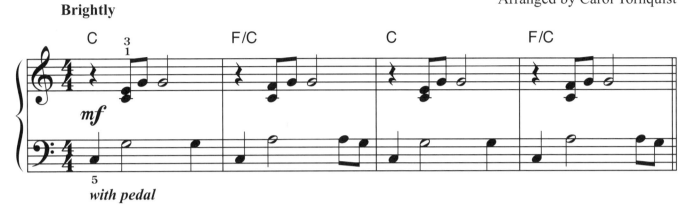

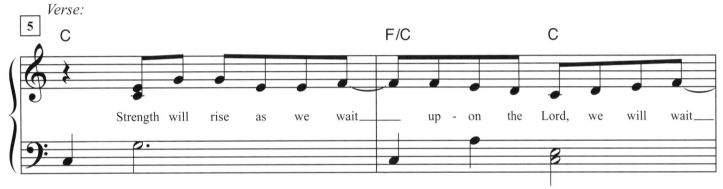

Strength will rise as we wait upon the Lord, we will wait

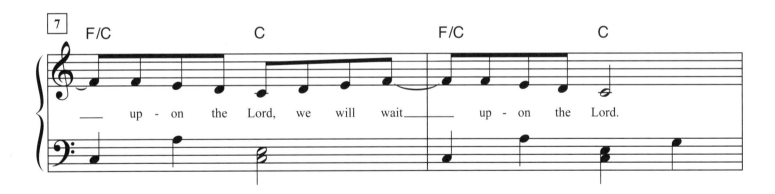

upon the Lord, we will wait upon the Lord.

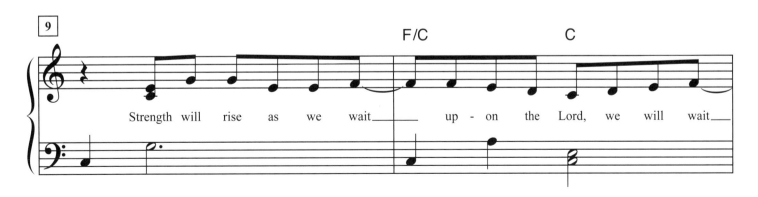

Strength will rise as we wait upon the Lord, we will wait

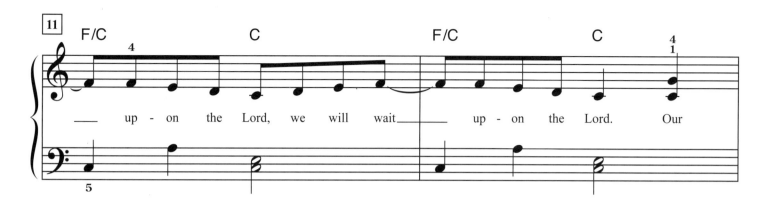

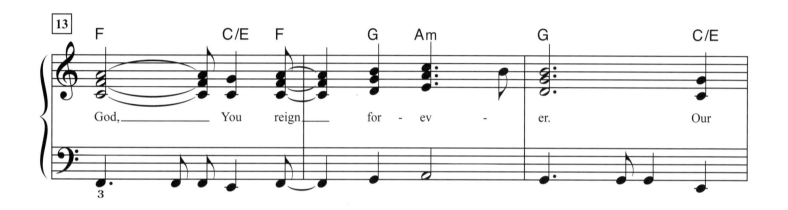

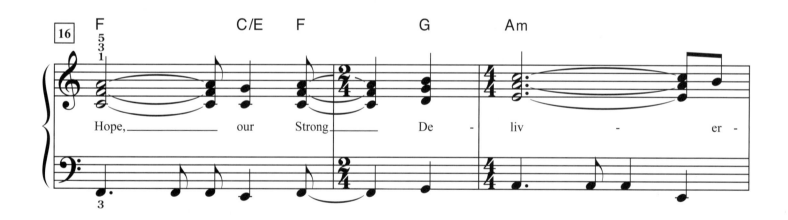

*Chorus:*

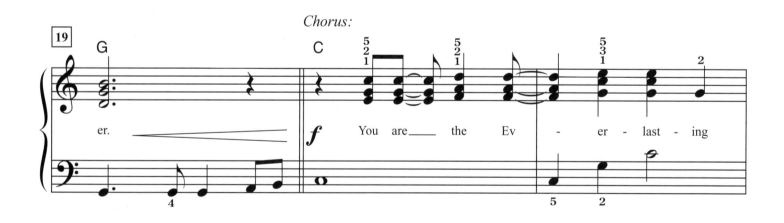

# CROWN HIM
# (MAJESTY)

Words and Music by Chris Tomlin,
Ed Cash and Matt Maher
Arranged by Carol Tornquist

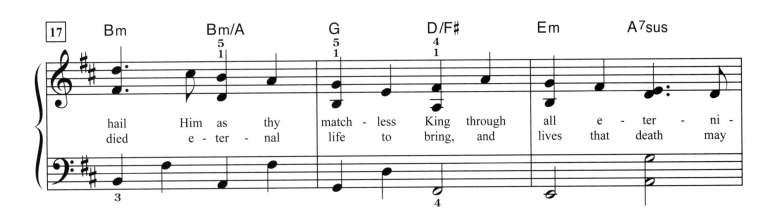

*Chorus:*

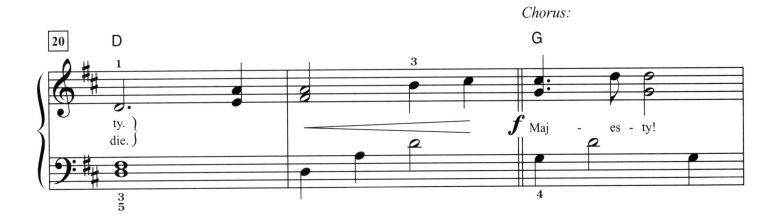

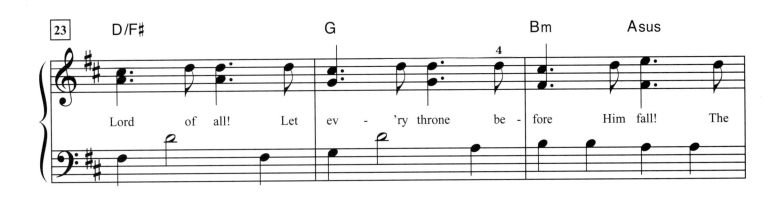

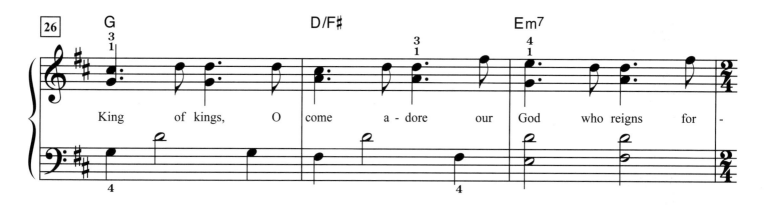

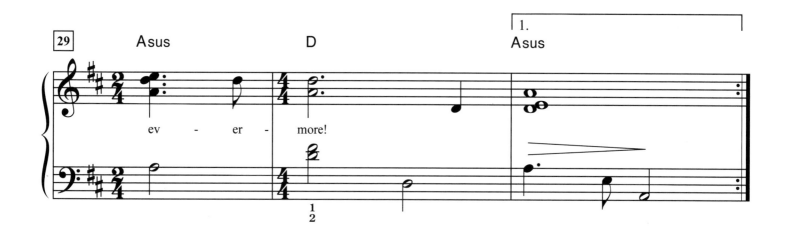

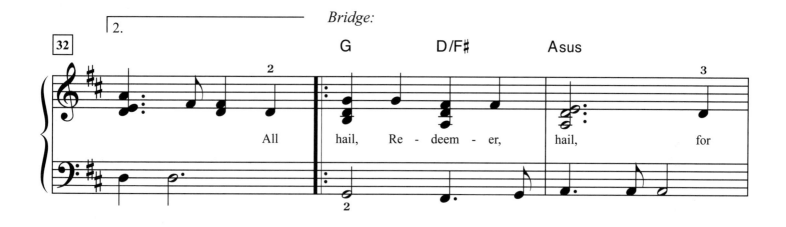

# CRY OUT TO JESUS

Words and Music by Brad Avery, David Carr,
Mac Powell, Mark Lee and Tai Anderson
Arranged by Carol Tornquist

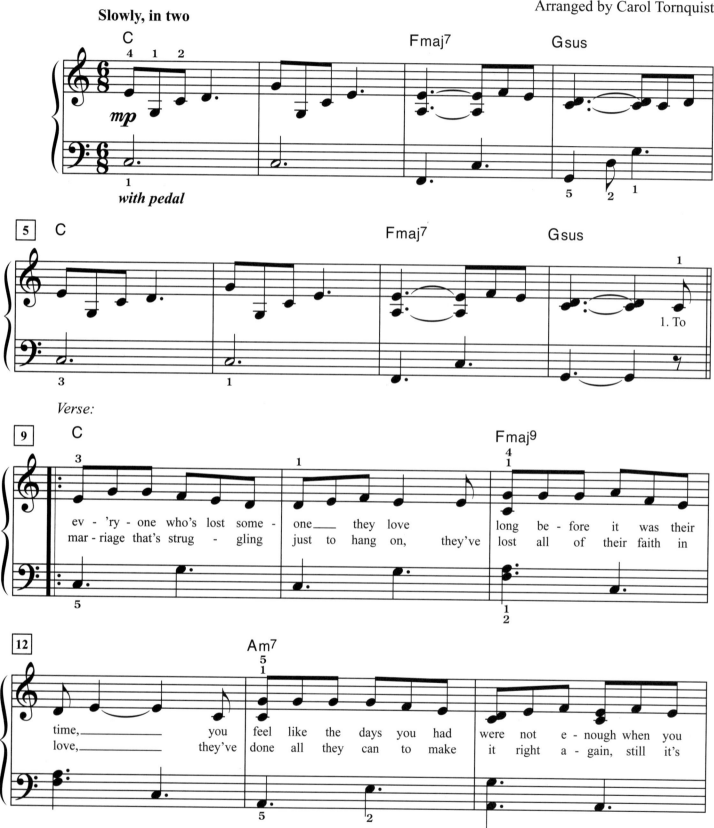

# EAST TO WEST

Words and Music by
Bernie Herms and Mark Hall
Arranged by Carol Tornquist

rest. I don't want to end up where___ You found me, and it ech - oes in___ my

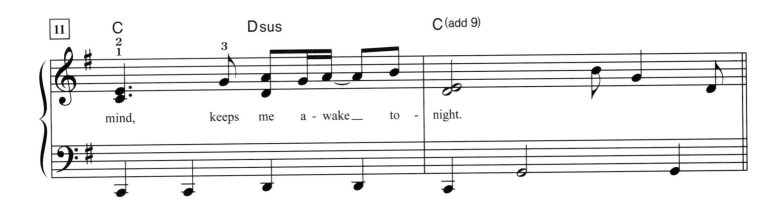

mind, keeps me a - wake___ to - night.

*Verse:*

2. I know You've cast my sin___ as far as the east is from the
3. *See additional lyrics.*

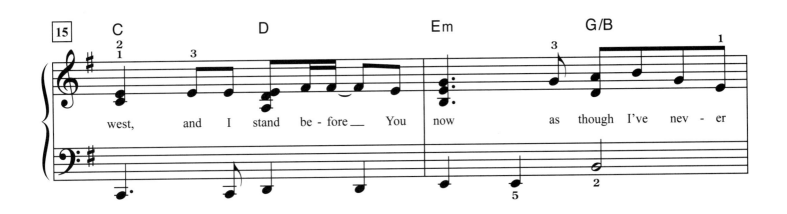

west, and I stand be - fore___ You now as though I've nev - er

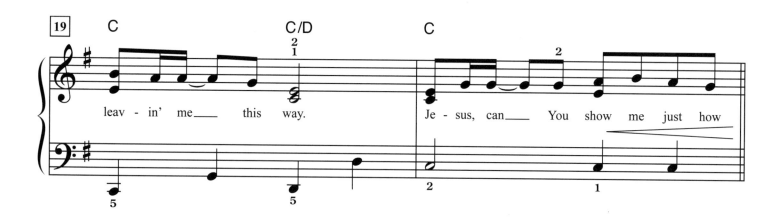

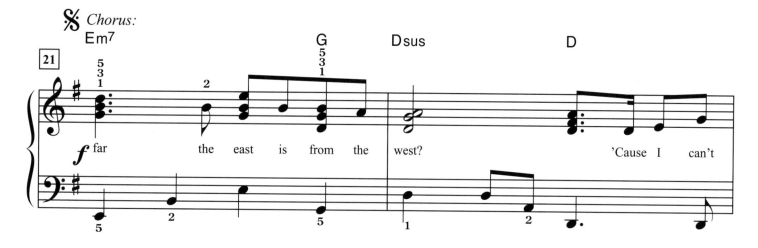

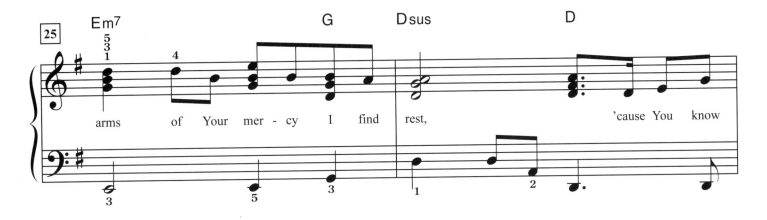

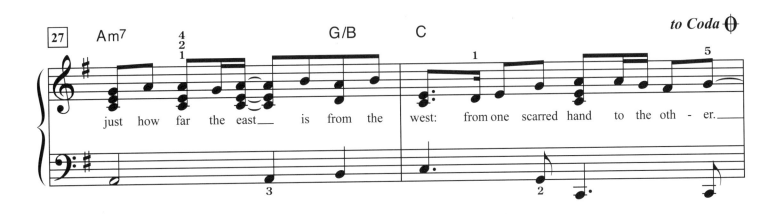

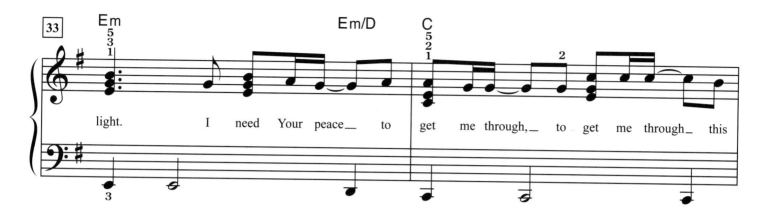

light. I need Your peace___ to get me through,___ to get me through___ this

night. I can't live by what I feel, but by the truth Your Word___ re-

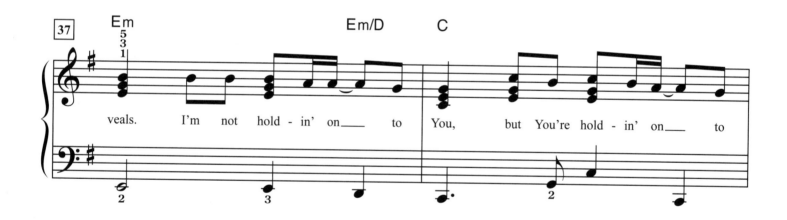

veals. I'm not hold-in' on___ to You, but You're hold-in' on___ to

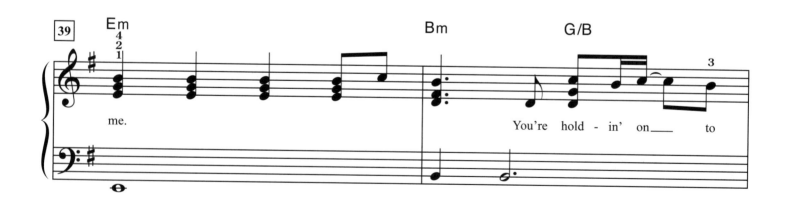

me. You're hold-in' on___ to

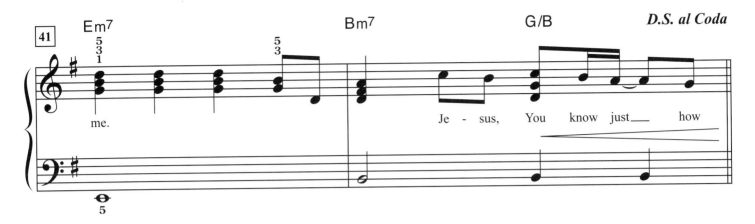

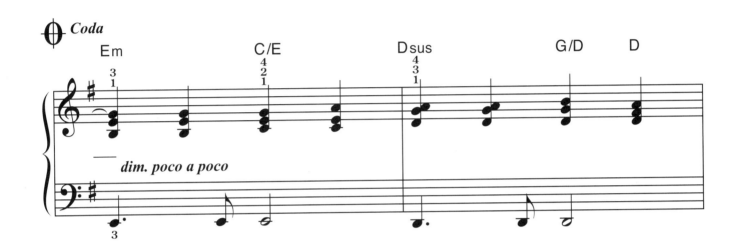

*Verse 3:*
I start the day, the war begins, endless reminding of my sin.
Time and time again Your truth is drowned out by the storm I'm in.
Today I feel like I'm just one mistake away from Your leavin' me this way.
*(To Chorus:)*

# FOREVER

Words and Music by Brian Johnson, Christa Black Gifford,
Gabe Wilson, Jenn Johnson, Joel Taylor and Kari Jobe
Arranged by Carol Tornquist

52

jah! The Lamb has o - ver - come. For - ev - er He is

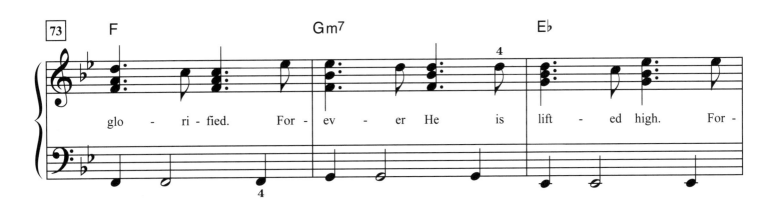

glo - ri - fied. For - ev - er He is lift - ed high. For -

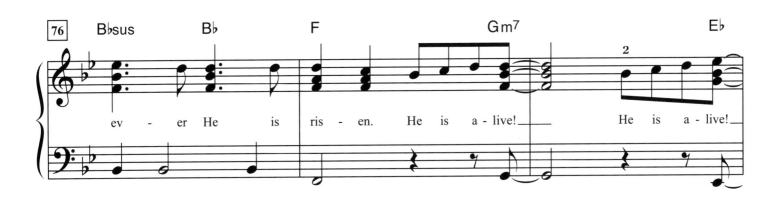

ev - er He is ris - en. He is a - live! He is a - live!

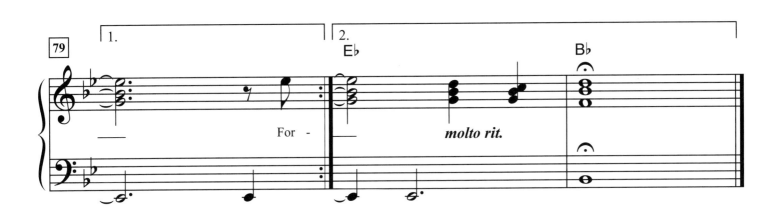

For - *molto rit.*

# FREE TO BE ME

Words and Music by
Francesca Battistelli
Arranged by Carol Tornquist

56

*Verse 3:*
Sometimes I believe that I can do anything,
Yet other times I think I've got nothing good to bring.
But You look at my heart and You tell me
That I've got all You seek, oh.
And it's easy to believe, even though
I've got a couple…
*(To Chorus:)*

# GLORIOUS DAY
# (LIVING HE LOVED ME)

Words and Music by
Mark Hall and Michael Bleecker
Arranged by Carol Tornquist

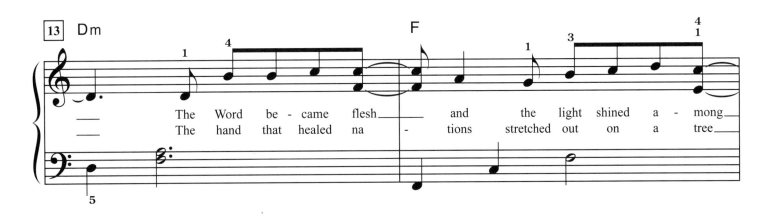

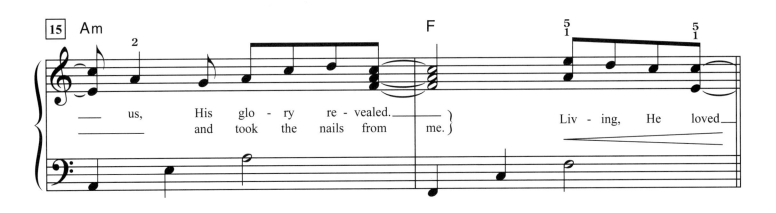

*Chorus:*

61

*Verse 3:*
One day the grave could conceal Him no longer.
One day the stone rolled away from the door.
Then He arose, over death He had conquered.
Now is ascended, my Lord evermore.
Death could not hold Him; the grave could not keep Him from rising again.
*(To Chorus:)*

# GOD'S NOT DEAD
# (LIKE A LION)

Words and Music by
Daniel Bashta
Arranged by Carol Tornquist

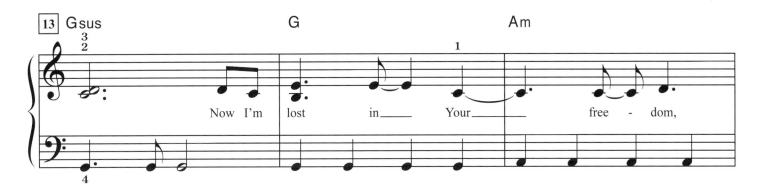

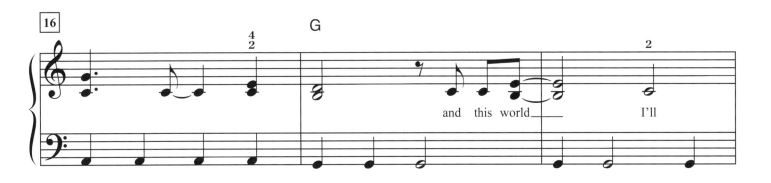

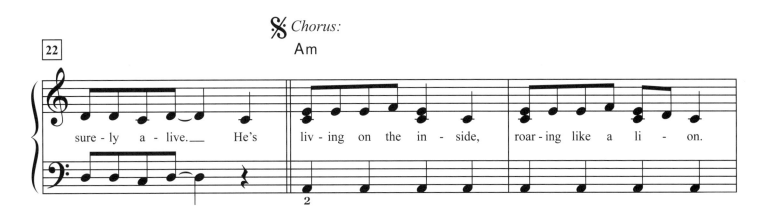

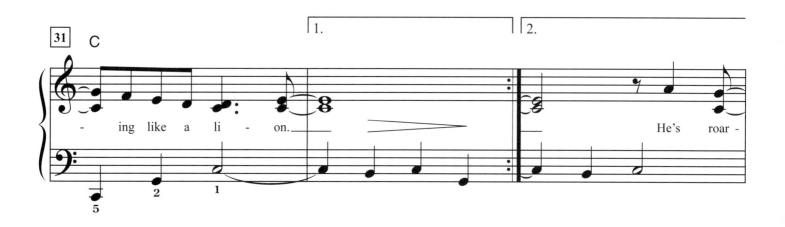

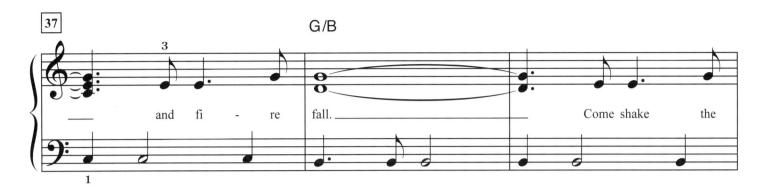

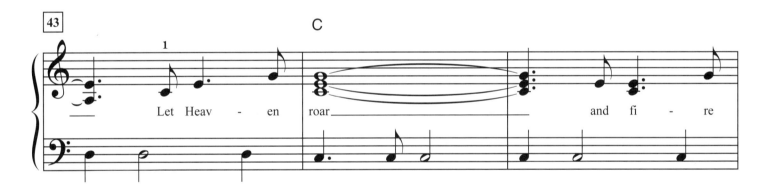

# GOOD MORNING

Words and Music by Aaron Rice, Cary Barlowe,
Jamie Moore, Mandisa Hundley and Toby McKeehan
Arranged by Carol Tornquist

Verse 2:
Slow down, breathe in, don't move ahead.
I'm just living in the moment.
I've got my arms raised, unphased, jump out of bed.
Gotta get this party going.
I went to bed dreaming.
You woke me up singing, "Get up, get up, hey!"
(To Chorus:)

# GREAT I AM

Words and Music by
Jared Anderson
Arranged by Carol Tornquist

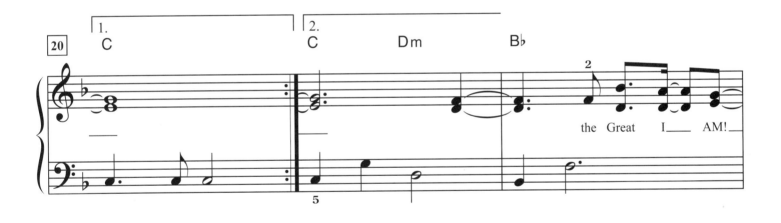

*Bridge:*

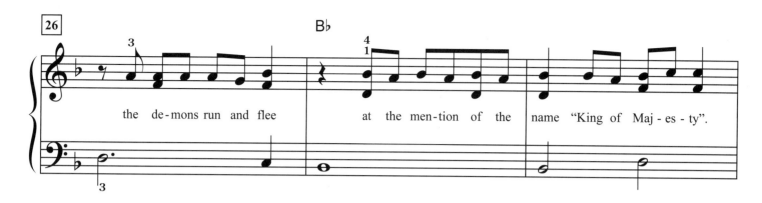

the de-mons run and flee at the men-tion of the name "King of Maj-es-ty".

There is no pow'r in hell or an-y who can stand be-fore the pow-er and the

pres-ence of the Great I__ AM,__ the Great I__ AM,__ the Great I__ AM.__

*Chorus:*

Hal - le - lu - jah! Ho - ly, ho - ly! God Al-might-

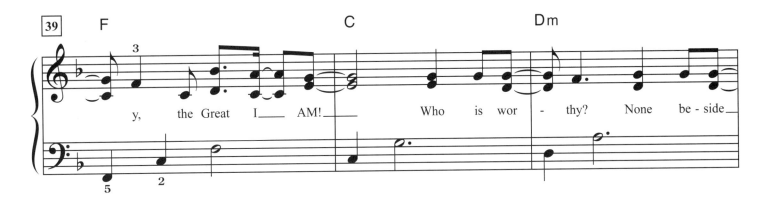

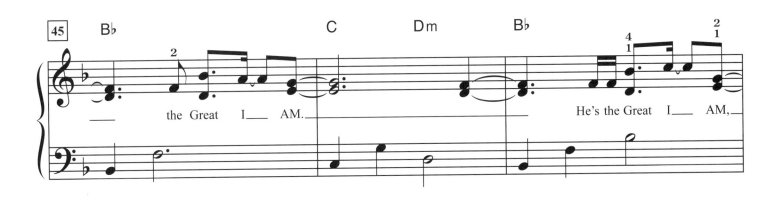

# HE REIGNS

Words and Music by
Peter Furler and Steve Taylor
Arranged by Carol Tornquist

**Moderately fast**

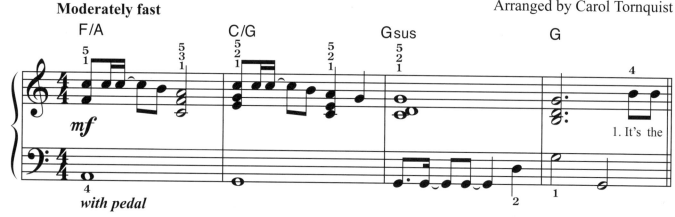

*with pedal*

*Verse:*

song of the\_\_ re-deemed\_\_
2. *See additional lyrics.*
ris-ing from\_ the Af-ri-can plain.

It's the song of the\_\_ for-giv-en drown-ing out\_\_ the Am-a-zon rain.

The song of A-sian\_ be-liev-ers

*Verse 2:*
Let it rise above the four winds, caught up in the heavenly sound.
Let praises echo from the towers of cathedrals to the faithful gathered underground.
Of all the songs sung from the dawn of creation, some were meant to persist.
Of all the bells rung from a thousand steeples, none rings truer than this:
*(To Chorus:)*

# HELLO, MY NAME IS

Words and Music by
Matthew West
Arranged by Carol Tornquist

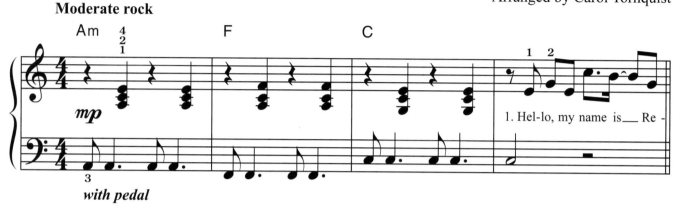

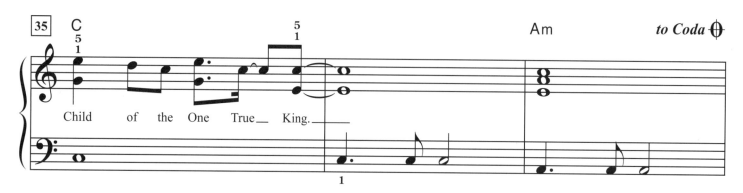

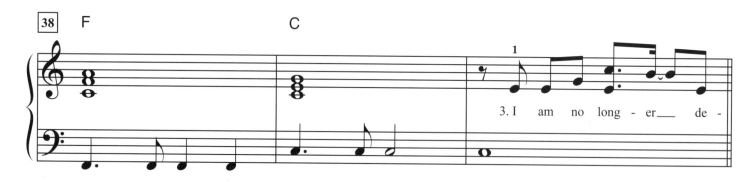

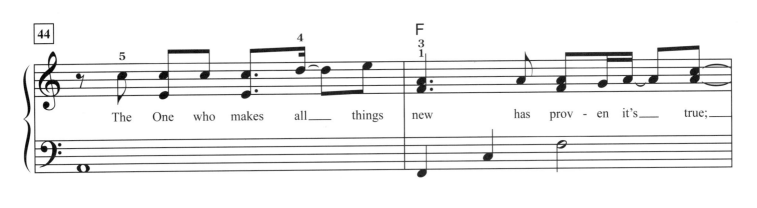

The One who makes all___ things new has prov-en it's___ true;___

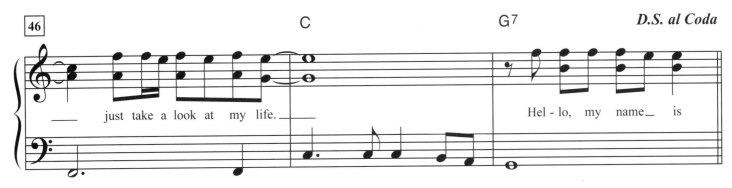

_D.S. al Coda_

___ just take a look at my life.___ Hel-lo, my name___ is

_Coda_

_Bridge:_

What love the

Fa-ther has lav-ished up-on us that we should be called___ His

chil-dren.___ I am a child of the one true___ King.___ What love the

# HOLY IS THE LORD

Words and Music by
Chris Tomlin and Louie Giglio
Arranged by Carol Tornquist

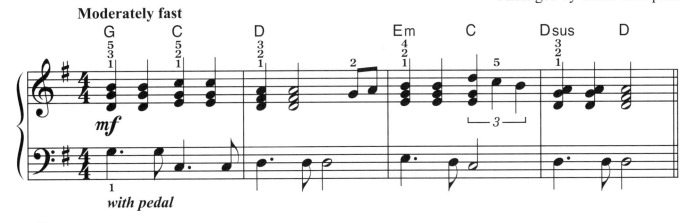

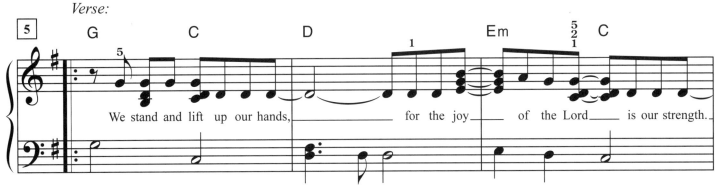

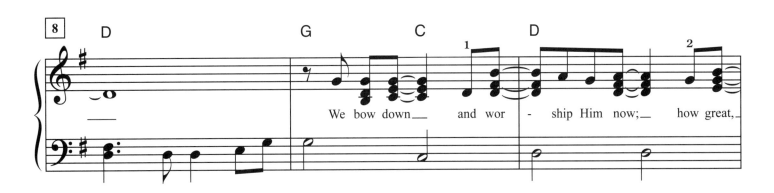

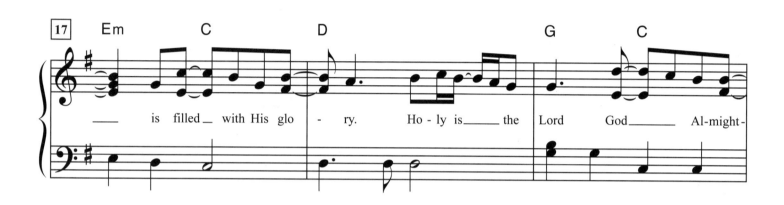

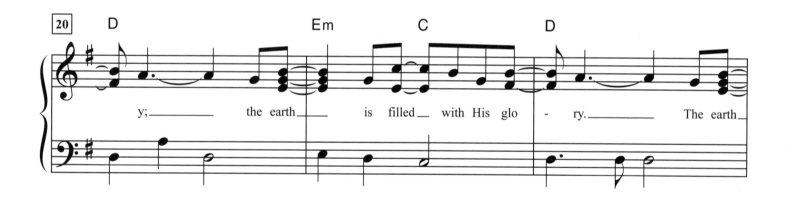

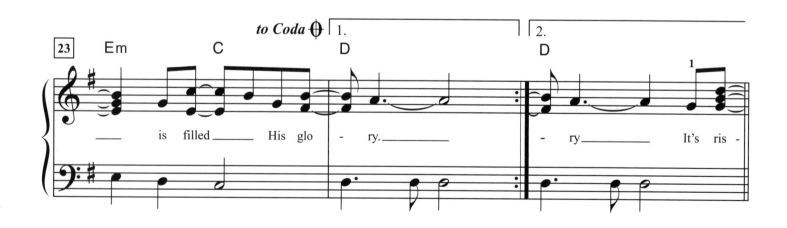

# HOLD ME

Words and Music by Chris Stevens,
Jamie Grace and Toby McKeehan
Arranged by Carol Tornquist

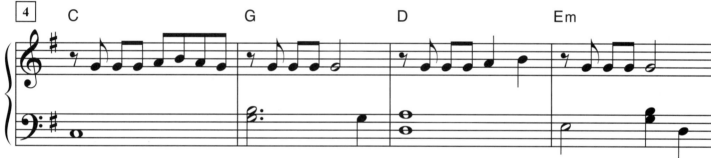

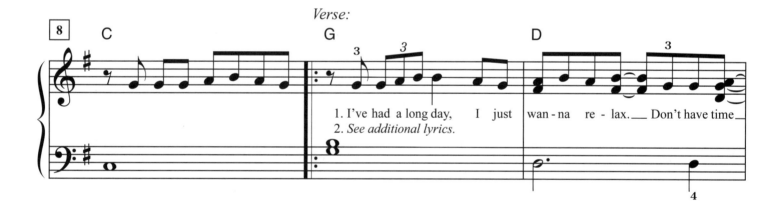

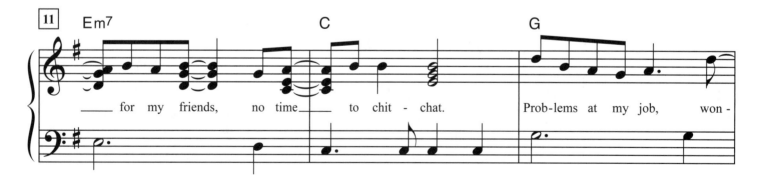

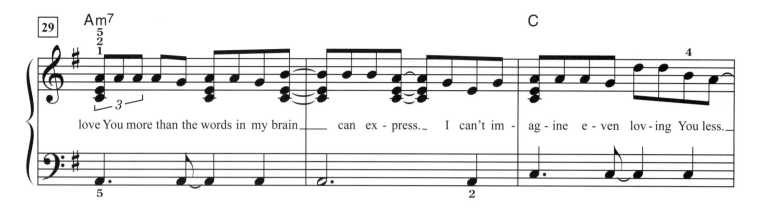

love You more than the words in my brain___ can ex - press.__ I can't im - ag - ine e - ven lov - ing You less.

___ Lord, I love the way You hold me.___ Whoa,___ oh, oh,___ oh,

___ oh,___ whoa.___ I love___ the way You hold___ me. Whoa,___

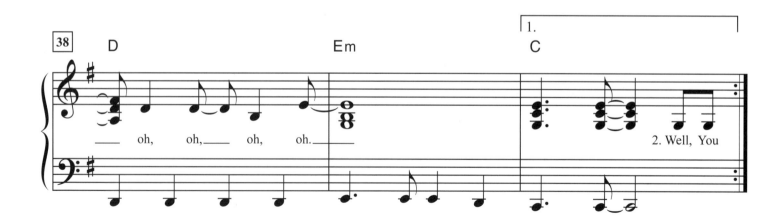

___ oh, oh,___ oh, oh.___ 2. Well, You

89

*Verse 2:*
Well, You took my day and You flipped it around,
Calmed the tidal wave and put my feet on the ground.
Forever in my heart, always on my mind,
It's crazy how I think about You all of the time.
And just when I think I'm 'bout to figure You out,
You make me wanna sing and shout.
*(To Chorus:)*

# HOW HE LOVES

Words and Music by
John Mark McMillan
Arranged by Carol Tornquist

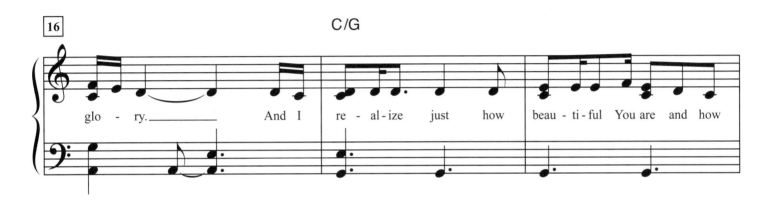

loves___ us,___ how He___ loves us___ all.___

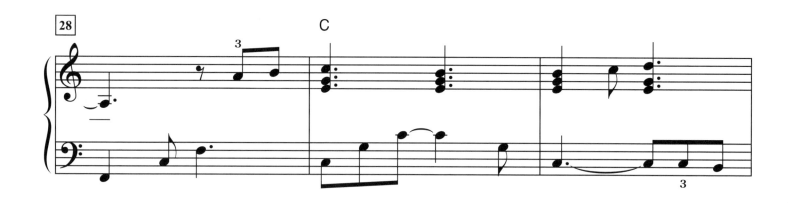

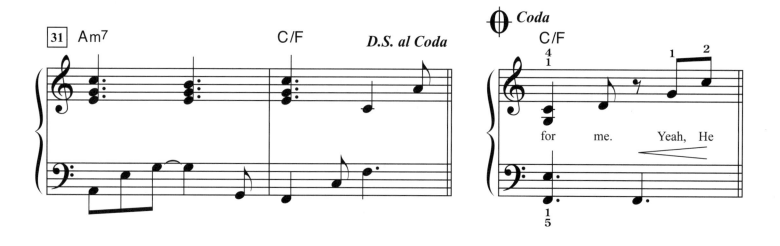

*D.S. al Coda*

*Coda*

for me. Yeah, He

*Chorus:*

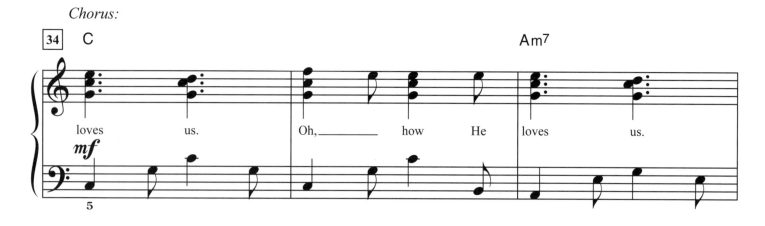

loves us. Oh,___ how He loves us.

Oh,_____ how He loves us. Oh,_____ how He

*Verse:*

loves. 3. And we are His por - tion and

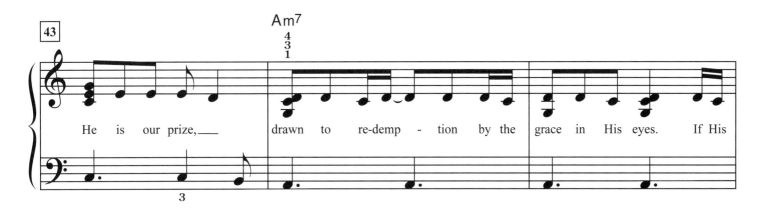

He is our prize,___ drawn to re-demp - tion by the grace in His eyes. If His

grace is an o - cean, we're all sink - ing._____

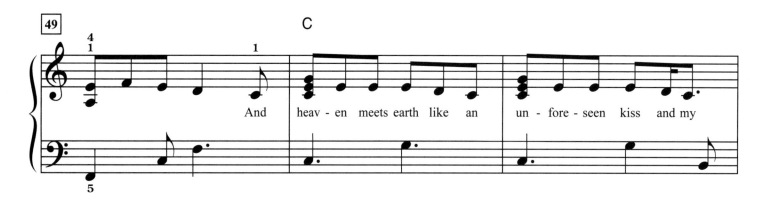

And heav-en meets earth like an un-fore-seen kiss and my

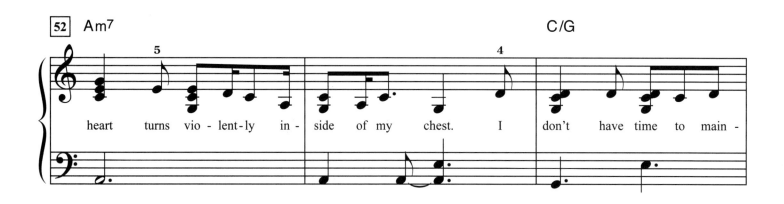

heart turns vio-lent-ly in-side of my chest. I don't have time to main-

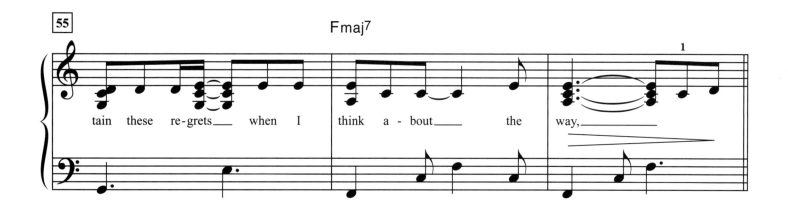

tain these re-grets____ when I think a-bout____ the way,____

*Chorus:*

Oh, how He____ loves us.____ Oh,

# I AM

Words and Music by
David Crowder and Ed Cash
Arranged by Carol Tornquist

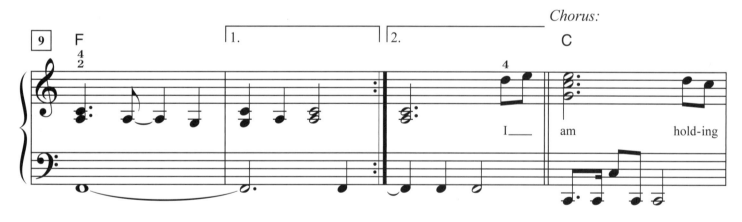

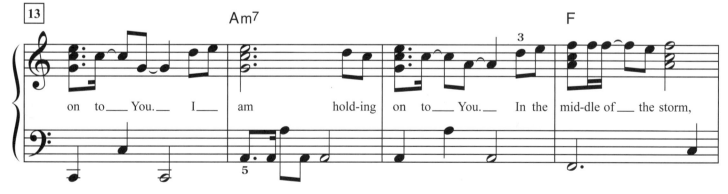

*Bridge:*

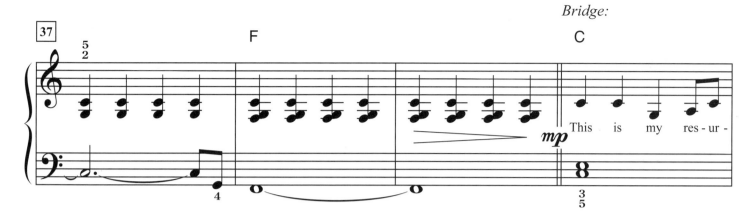

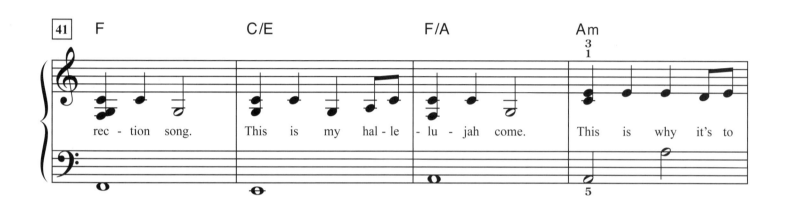

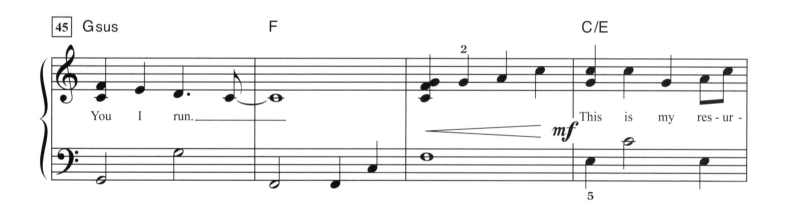

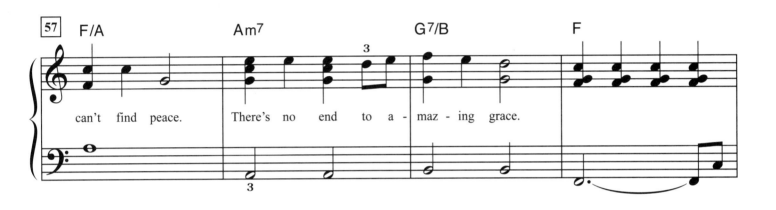

*Chorus:*

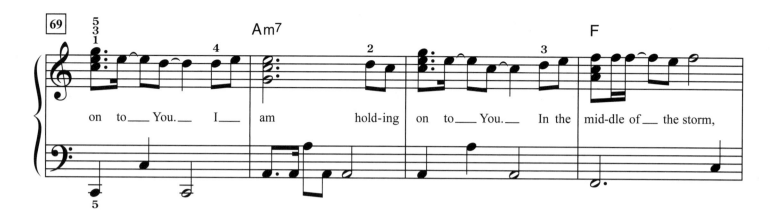

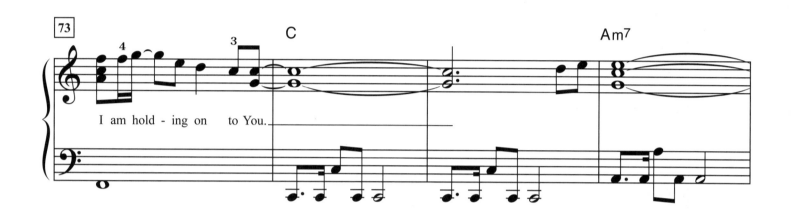

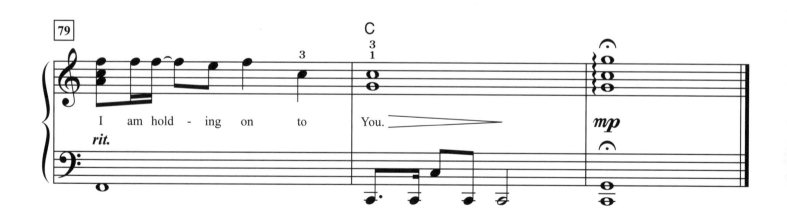

# I NEED A MIRACLE

Words and Music by David Carr,
Mac Powell, Mark Lee and Tai Anderson
Arranged by Carol Tornquist

*Verse 2:*
He lost his job and all he had in the fall of '09.
Now he feared the worst, that he would lose his children and his wife.
So he drove down deep into the woods and thought he'd end it all,
And prayed, "Lord above, I need a miracle."
*(To Chorus:)*

*Verse 3:*
He turned on the radio to hear a song for the last time.
He didn't know what he was looking for or even what he'd find.
And the song he heard, it gave him hope and strength to carry on.
And on that night they found a miracle.
*(To Chorus:)*

# I WILL RISE

Words and Music by Chris Tomlin,
Jesse Reeves, Louie Giglio and Matt Maher
Arranged by Carol Tornquist

**Moderately slow**

*Verse:*

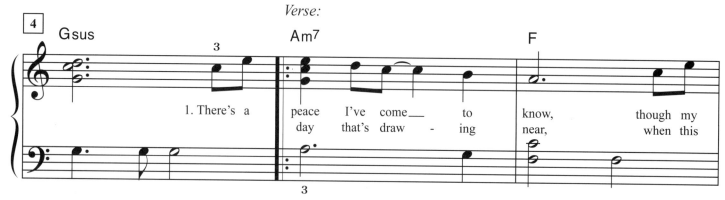

1. There's a peace I've come to know, though my
   day that's draw - ing near, when this

heart and flesh may fail. There's an an - chor for my
dark - ness breaks to light, and the sha - dows dis - ap -

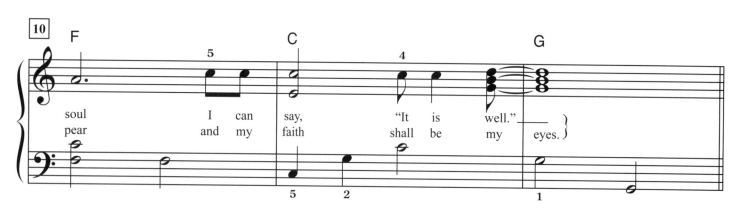

soul I can say, "It is well." 
pear and my faith shall be my eyes.

# JESUS, FRIEND OF SINNERS

Words and Music by
Matthew West and Mark Hall
Arranged by Carol Tornquist

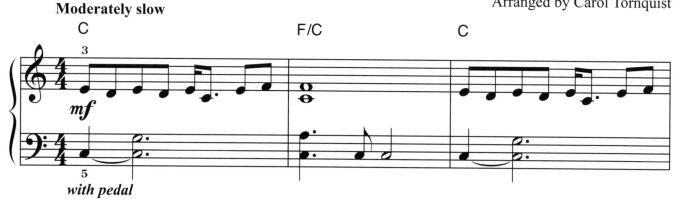

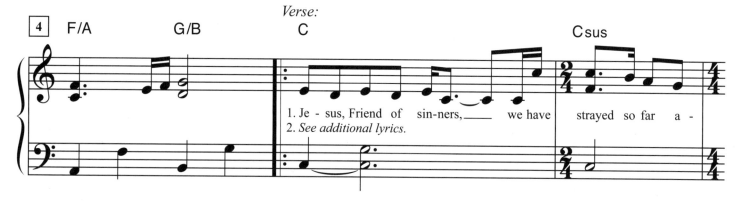

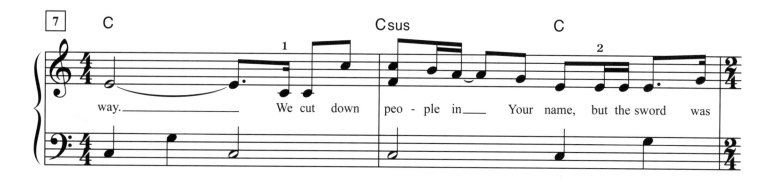

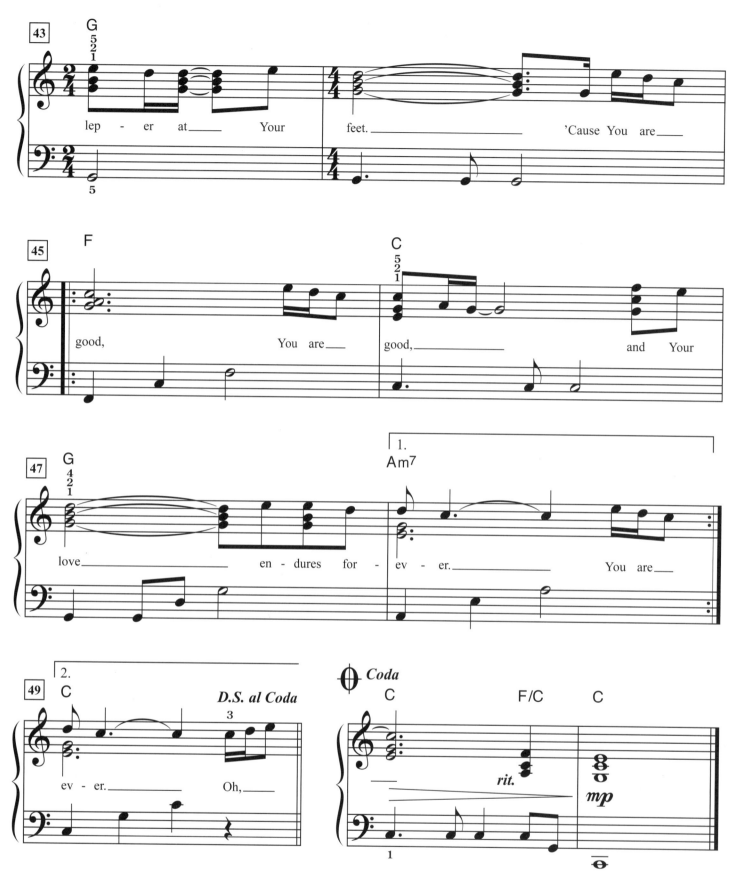

*Verse 2:*
Jesus, Friend of sinners, the One whose writing in the sand
Made the righteous turn away and the stones fall from their hands,
Help us to remember we are all the least of these.
Let the memory of Your mercy bring Your people to their knees.
Nobody knows what we're for, only what we're against when we judge the wounded.
What if we put down our signs, crossed over the lines and loved like You did?
*(To Chorus:)*

# LORD, I NEED YOU

Words and Music by Christy Nockels, Daniel Carson,
Jesse Reeves, Kristian Stanfill and Matt Maher
*Arranged by Carol Tornquist*

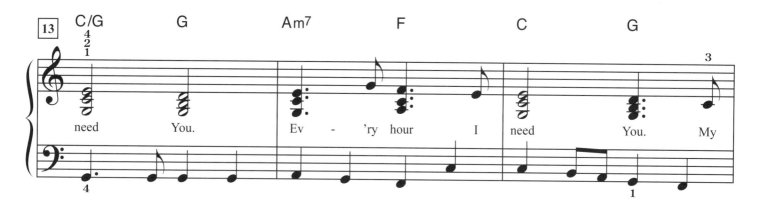

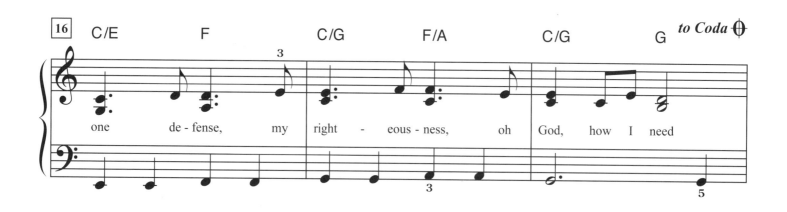

*Bridge:*

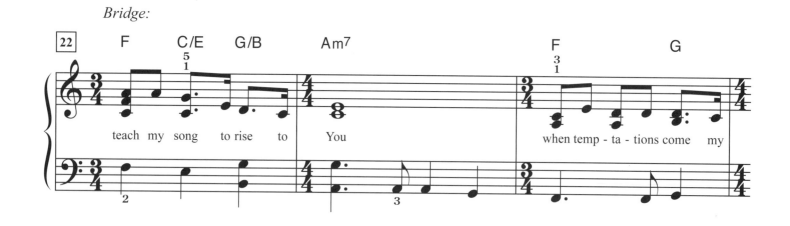

# MAN OF SORROWS

Words and Music by
Brooke Ligertwood and Matt Crocker
Arranged by Carol Tornquist

**Slowly and steadily**

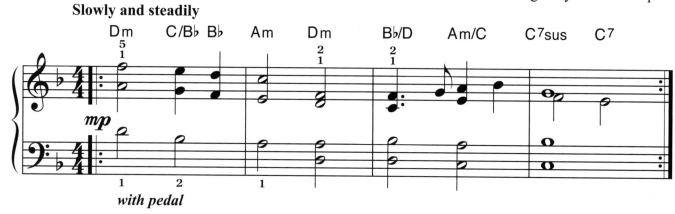

*with pedal*

*Verse:*

1. Man of sor - rows, Lamb of God, by His own be -

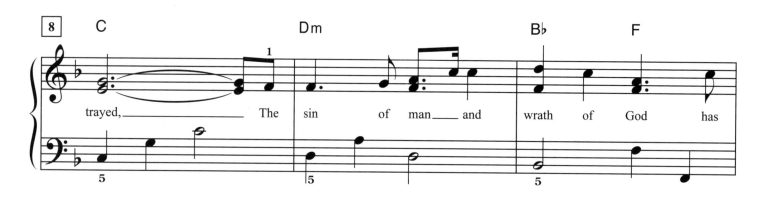

trayed,_____ The sin of man___ and wrath of God has

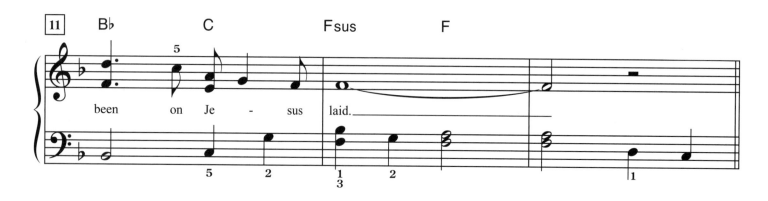

been on Je - sus laid._____

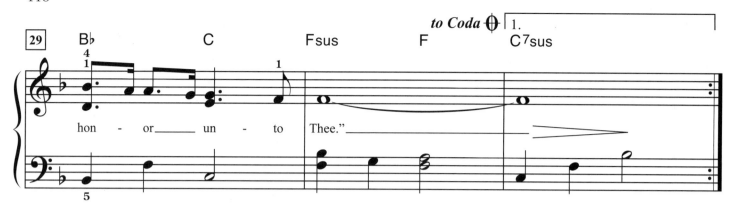

hon - or_____ un - to Thee."_____

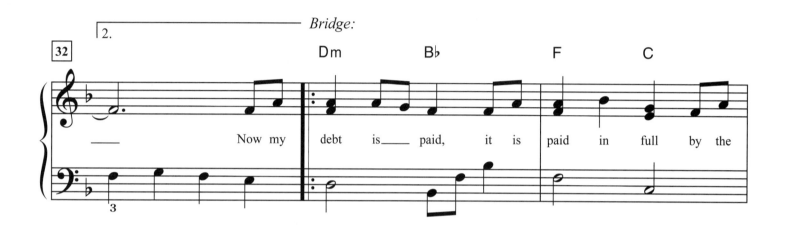

*Bridge:*

_____ Now my debt is____ paid, it is paid in full by the

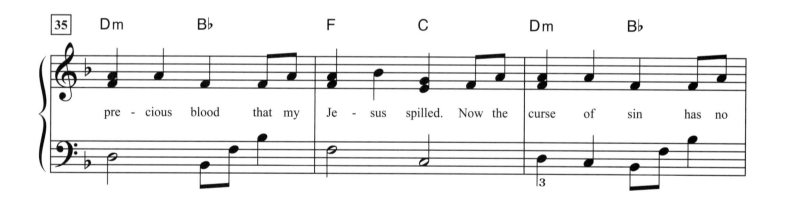

pre - cious blood that my Je - sus spilled. Now the curse of sin has no

hold on me. Whom the Son sets free, oh, is free in - deed. Now my

*Verse 3:*
Sent of heaven, God's own Son, to purchase and redeem,
And reconcile the very ones who nailed Him to that tree.
*(To Chorus:)*

*Verse 4:*
See, the stone is rolled away, behold the empty tomb.
Hallelujah, God be praised, He's risen from the grave.
*(To Chorus:)*

# MY SAVIOR, MY GOD

Words and Music by
Aaron Shust and Dora Greenwell
Arranged by Carol Tornquist

*Chorus:*

# ONE THING REMAINS
## (YOUR LOVE NEVER FAILS)

Words and Music by Jeremy Riddle,
Brian Johnson and Christa Black
Arranged by Carol Tornquist

124

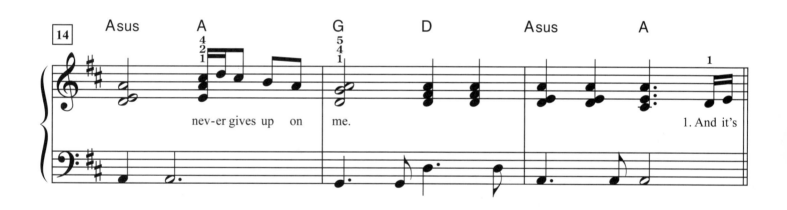

*Verse:*

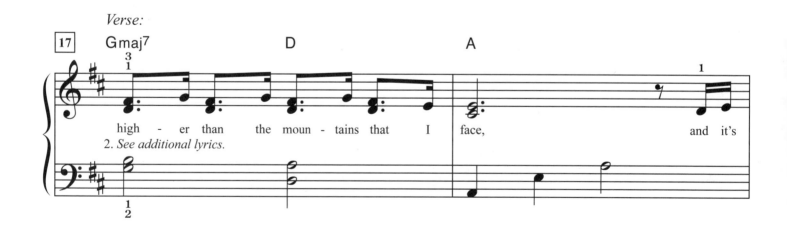

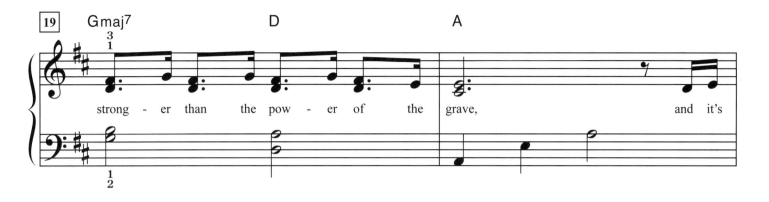

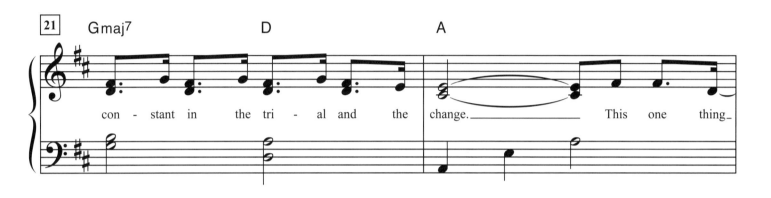

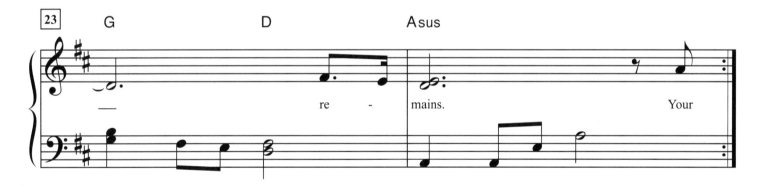

*Chorus:*

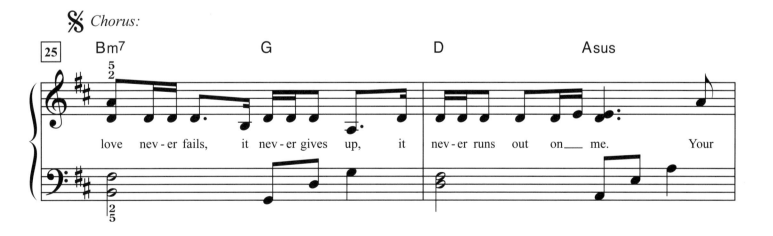

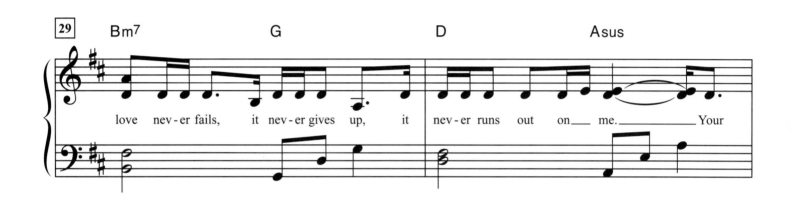

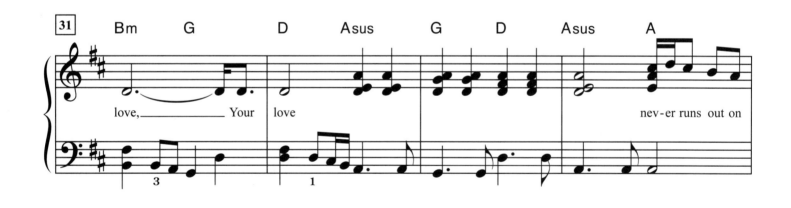

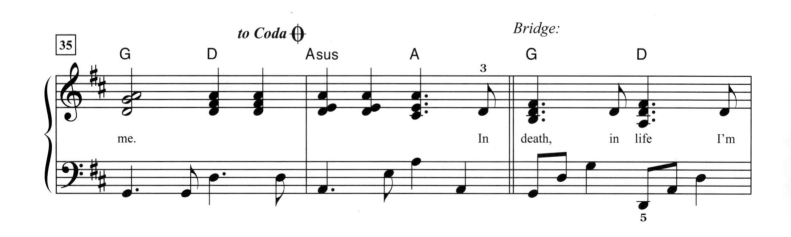

*Verse 2:*
And on and on and on and on it goes.
Yes, it overwhelms and satisfies my soul.
And I'll never, ever have to be afraid.
This one thing remains.
*(To Chorus:)*

# OCEANS
# (WHERE FEET MAY FAIL)

Words and Music by Joel Houston,
Matt Crocker and Salomon Ligthelm
Arranged by Carol Tornquist

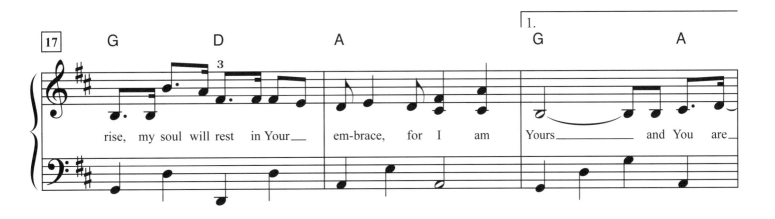

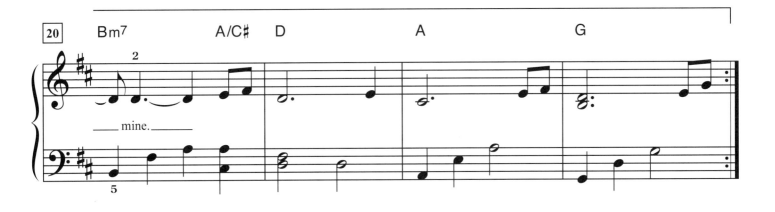

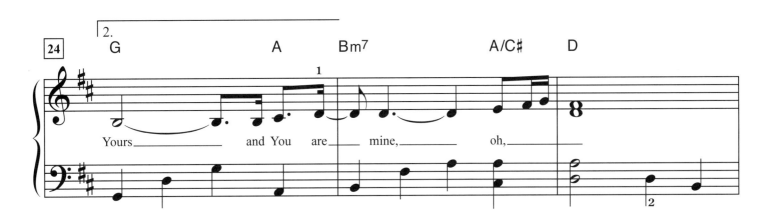

And You are_____ mine,_____ oh.

*Bridge:*

Spir-it, lead me where____ my trust is with - out bor-ders. Let me walk up-on____ the wa-ters wher-

ev - er You____ would call me. Take me deep-er than____ my feet could ev - er wan-der, and my

# ONLY HOPE

Words and Music by
Jonathan Foreman
Arranged by Carol Tornquist

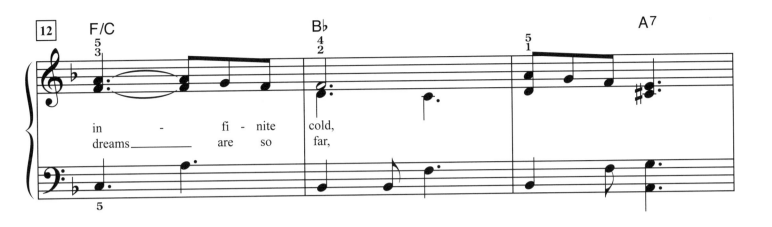

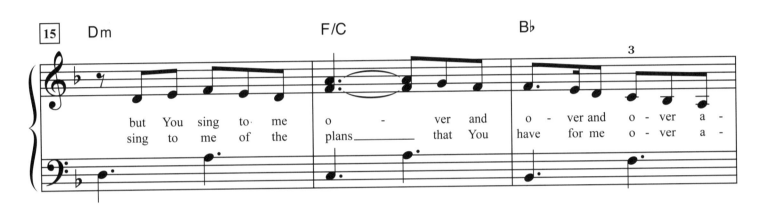

*Chorus:*

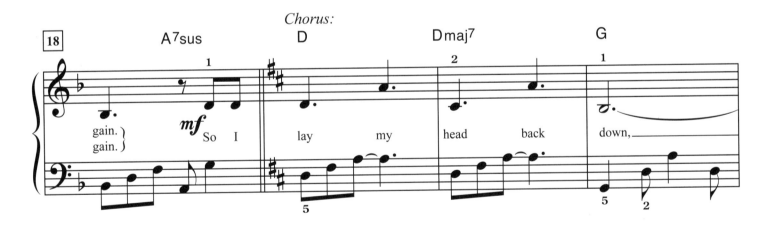

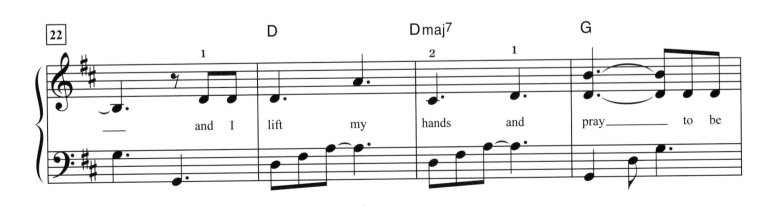

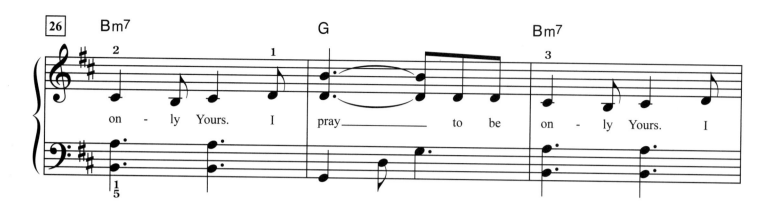

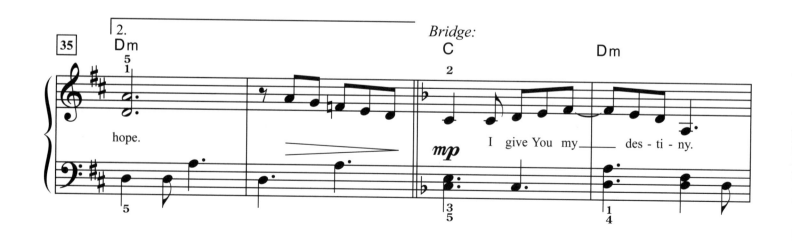

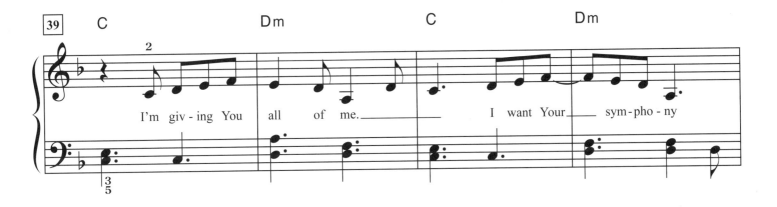

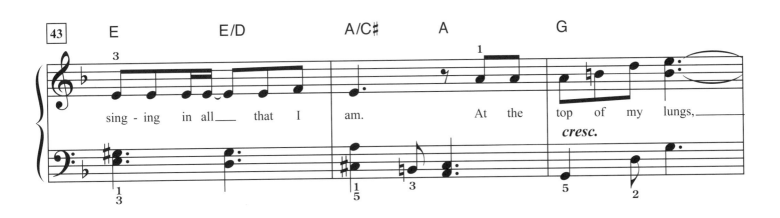

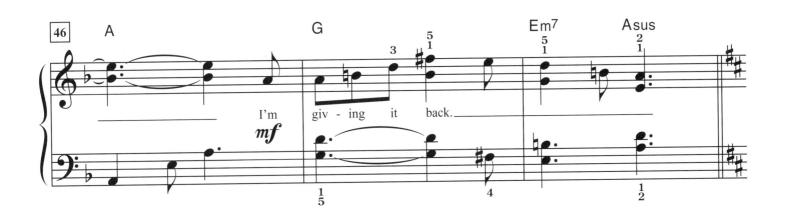

*Chorus:*

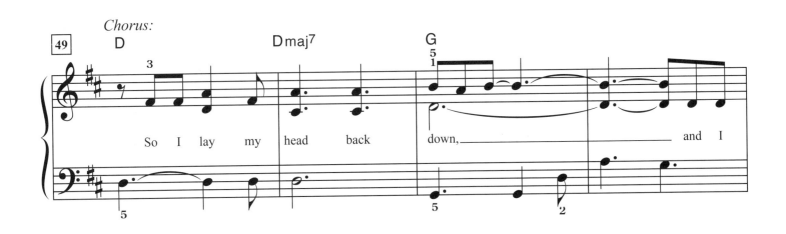

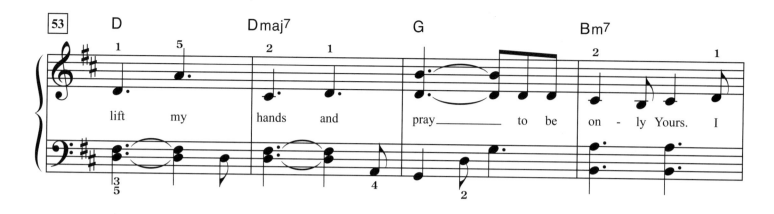

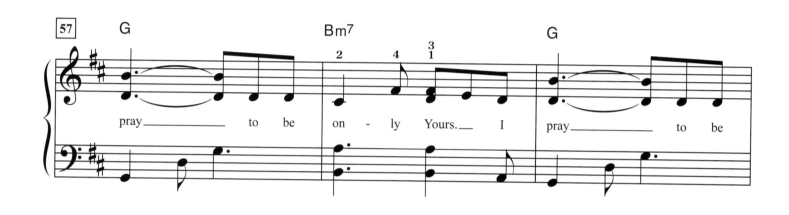

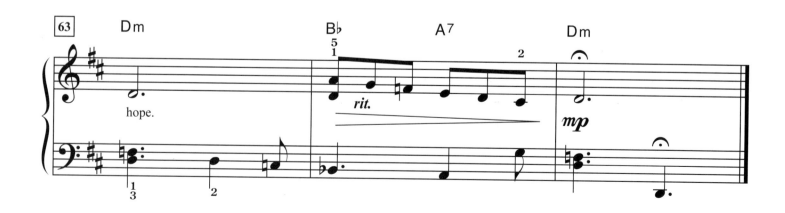

# THE ONLY NAME
# (YOURS WILL BE)

Words and Music by
Benji Cowart
Arranged by Carol Tornquist

138

# OVERCOMER

Words and Music by Ben Glover,
Chris Stevens and David Garcia
Arranged by Carol Tornquist

Verse:

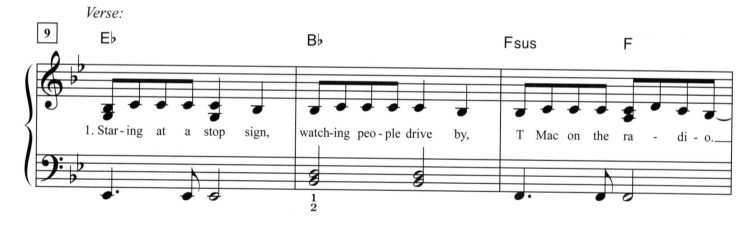

looking for a ray of hope. Ooh

whatever it is you may be going through, ooh

I know He's not gonna let it get the best of you.

*%S Chorus:*

You're an overcomer! Stay in the fight

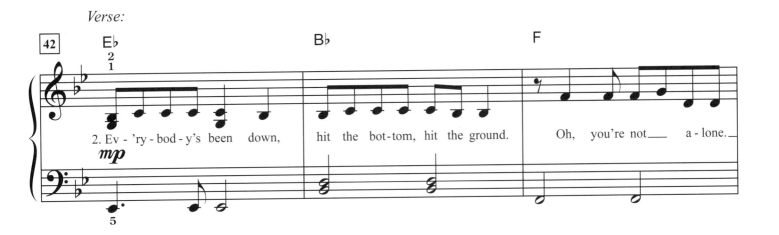

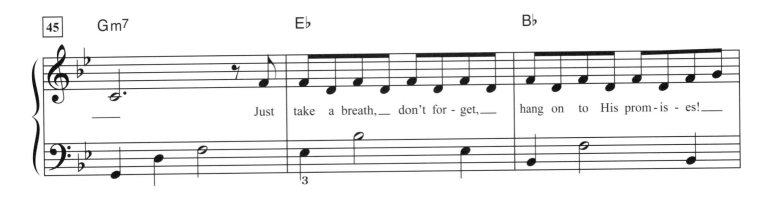

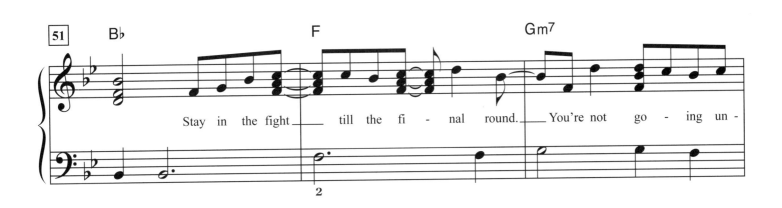

144

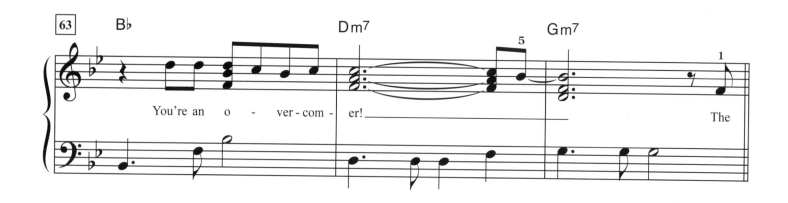

# THE PROOF OF YOUR LOVE

Words and Music by Luke Smallbone, Joel David Smallbone,
Ben Glover, Frederick Williams, Jonathan Lee and Mia Fieldes
Arranged by Carol Tornquist

*Verse:*

give to a need-y soul but don't have love, then who is poor? It

seems all the pov-er-ty is found in me. So

*Chorus:*

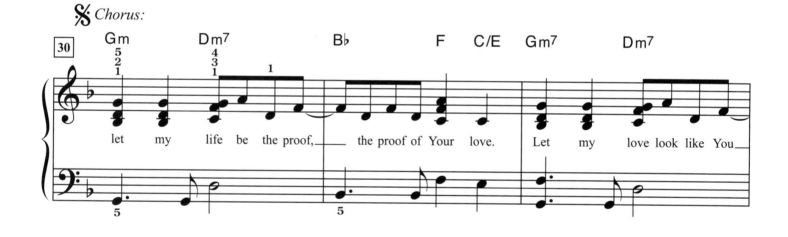

let my life be the proof, the proof of Your love. Let my love look like You

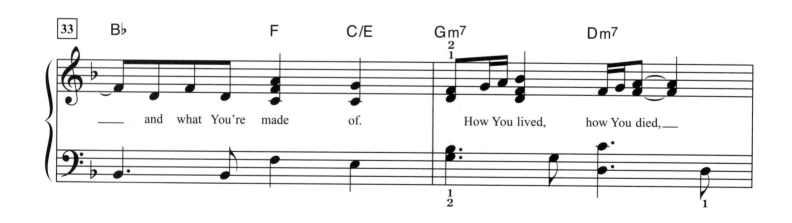

and what You're made of. How You lived, how You died,

love is sac - ri -fice. So let my life be the proof, the proof of Your love.

*Bridge:*

Whoa, when it's all said and done, whoa,

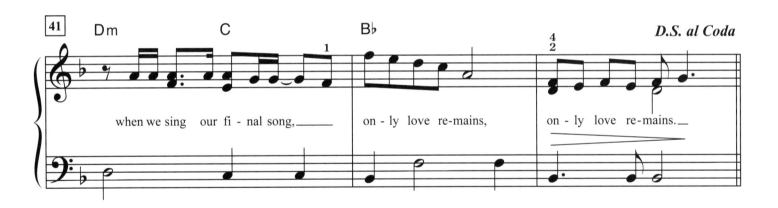

when we sing our fi - nal song, on - ly love re-mains, on - ly love re-mains.

*Coda*

# REDEEMED

Words and Music by
Benji Cowart and Michael Weaver
Arranged by Carol Tornquist

# REVELATION SONG

Words and Music by
Jennie Lee Riddle
Arranged by Carol Tornquist

**Slowly and steadily**

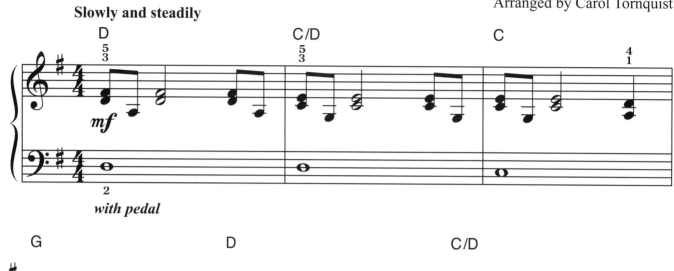

*Verse:*

1. Wor - thy is the
2., 3. *See additional lyrics.*

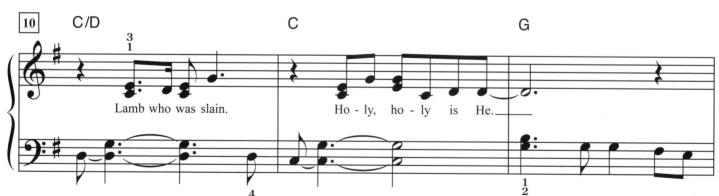

Lamb who was slain.　Ho - ly, ho - ly is He.

come.   With all cre-a-tion I sing   praise to the King of kings.

You are my ev-'ry-thing, and   I will a-dore You.

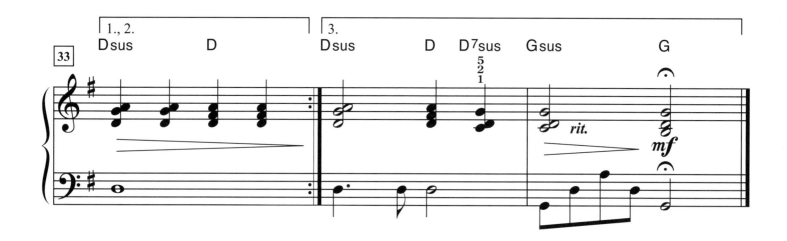

*Verse 2:*
Clothed in rainbows of living color,
Flashes of lightning, rolls of thunder,
Blessing and honor, strength and glory and power
Be to You, the only wise King.
*(To Chorus:)*

*Verse 3:*
Filled with wonder, awestruck wonder,
At the mention of Your name.
Jesus, Your name is power, breath, and living water,
Such a marvelous mystery.
*(To Chorus:)*

# SPEAK LIFE

Words and Music by Jamie Moore,
Ryan Stevenson and Toby McKeehan
Arranged by Carol Tornquist

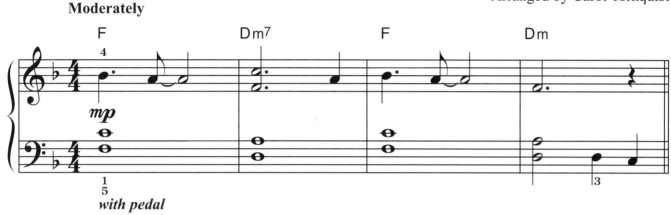

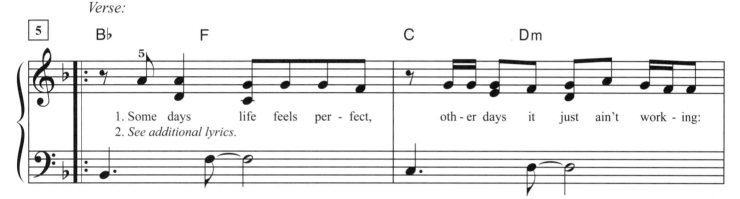

1. Some days life feels per-fect, oth-er days it just ain't work-ing:
2. *See additional lyrics.*

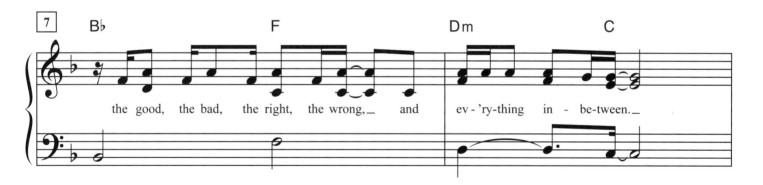

the good, the bad, the right, the wrong,__ and ev-'ry-thing in-be-tween.__

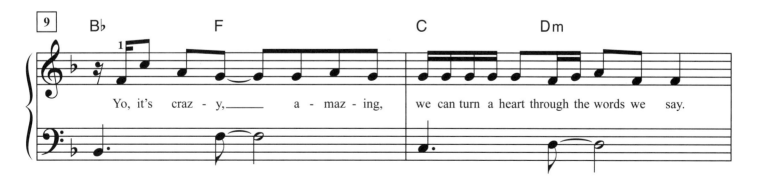

Yo, it's craz-y,__ a-maz-ing, we can turn a heart through the words we say.

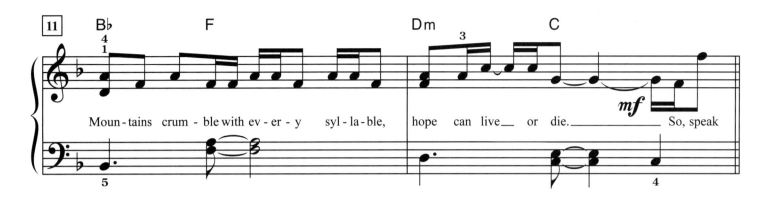

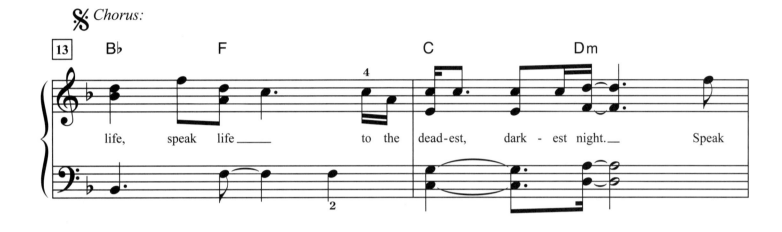

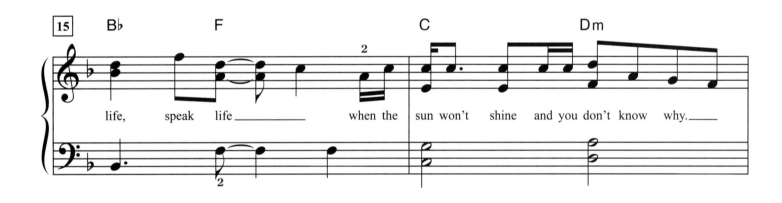

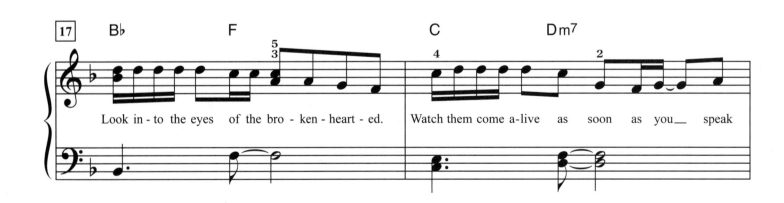

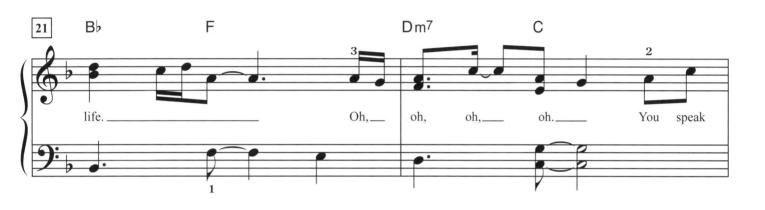

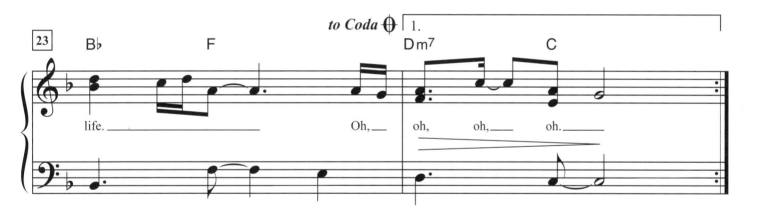

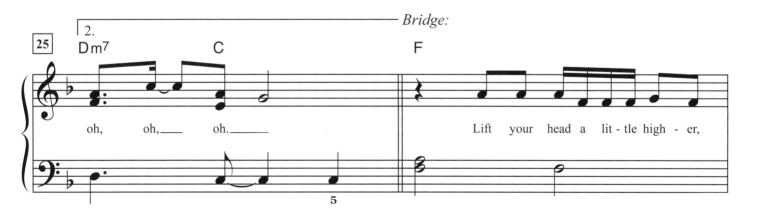

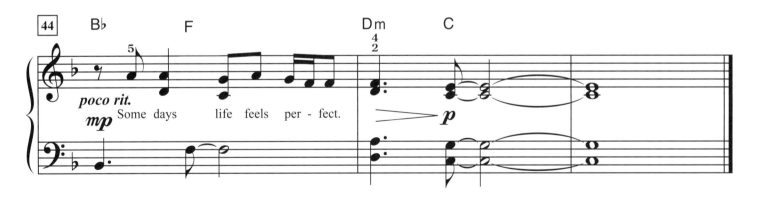

*Verse 2:*
Some days the tongue gets twisted,
Other days my thoughts just fall apart.
I do, I don't, I will, I won't.
It's like I'm drowning in the deep.
Well, it's crazy to imagine words from our lips
As the arms of compassion.
Mountains crumble with every syllable.
Hope can live or die.
*(To Chorus;)*

# SHAKE

Words and Music by Bart Millard, Ben Glover,
David Garcia and Solomon Olds
Arranged by Carol Tornquist

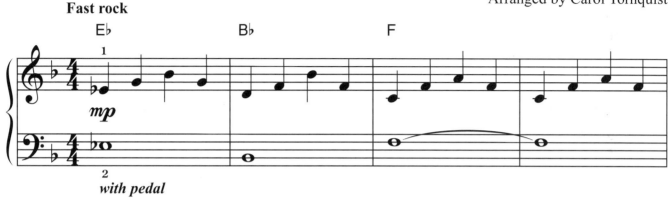

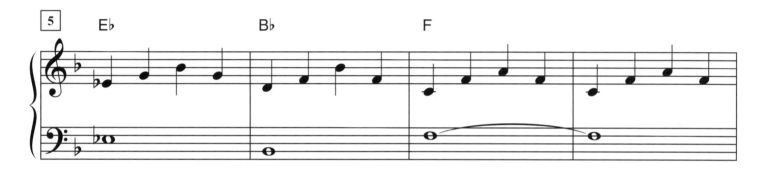

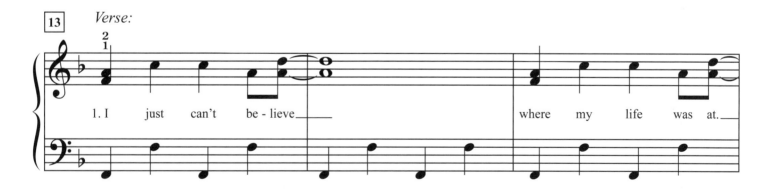

Verse 2:
Maybe He came to you when everything seemed fine,
Or maybe your world was upside down,
It hit you right between the eye, eye, eyes.
No matter when it happened, at seven or ninety-five,
Move your feet, 'cause you are free,
And you've never been more alive.
(To Chorus:)

# STRONG TOWER

Words and Music by Aaron Sprinkle,
Jon Micah Sumrall, Marc Byrd and Mark Lee
Arranged by Carol Tornquist

# TAKE ME TO THE KING

Words and Music by
Kirk Franklin
Arranged by Carol Tornquist

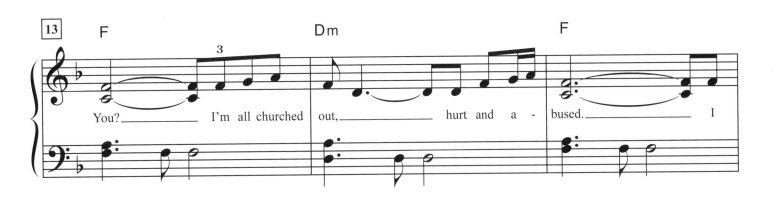

soul re-fus-es to\_\_ die._____ One touch will change my\_\_

*Chorus:*

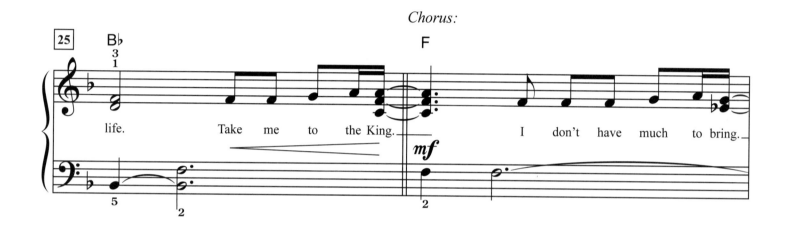

life. Take me to the King. I don't have much to bring.\_\_

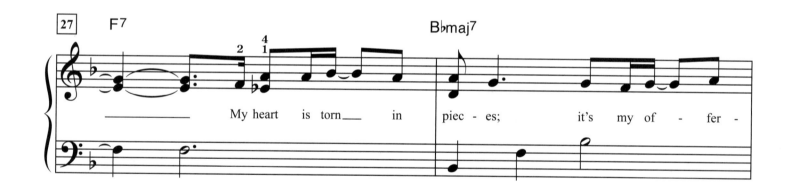

_____ My heart is torn\_\_ in piec - es; it's my of - fer -

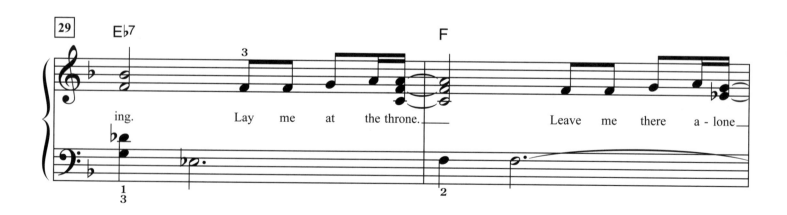

ing. Lay me at the throne.\_\_ Leave me there a - lone\_\_

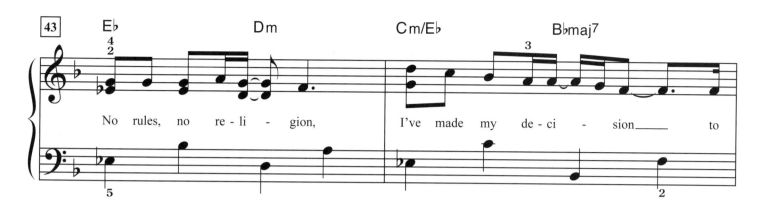

Chorus:

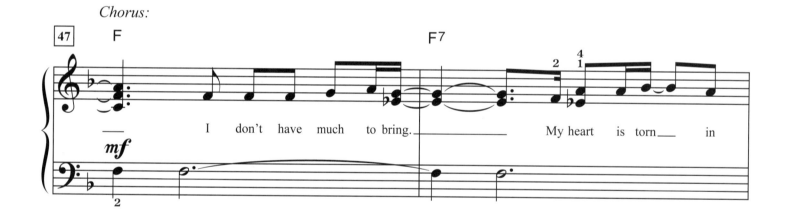

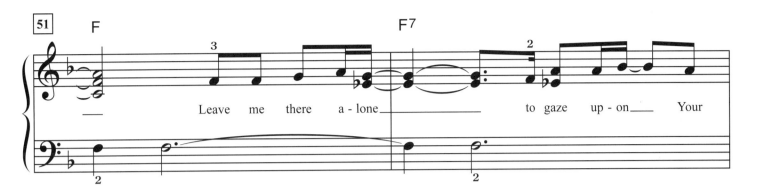

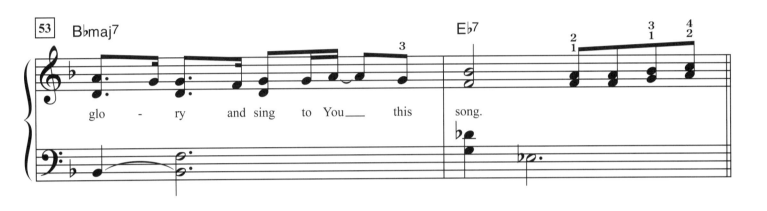

*Bridge:*

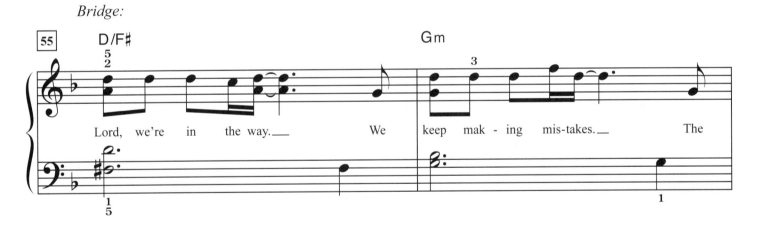

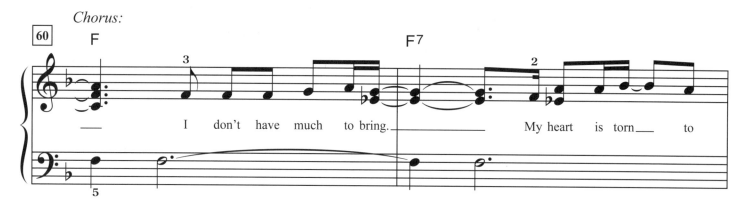

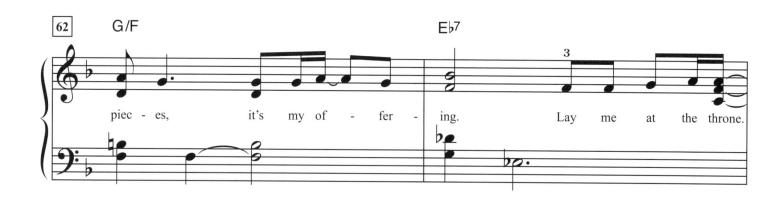

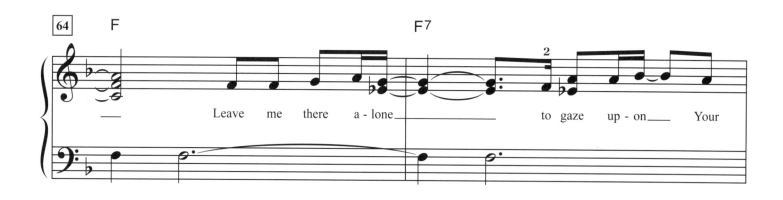

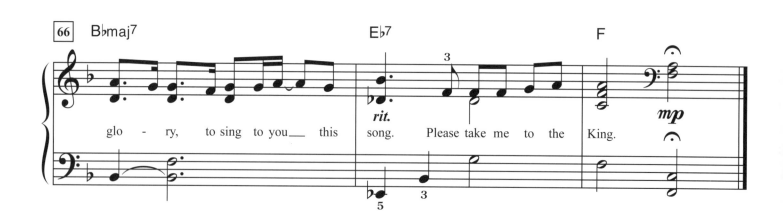

# THERE WILL BE A DAY

Words and Music by
Jeremy Camp
Arranged by Carol Tornquist

**Verse:**

1. I try to hold__ on to this world with ev - 'ry - thing__ I
2. See additional lyrics.

have, but I feel the weight__ of what it brings, and the hurt that tries__ to

grab. The man - y trials that seem__ to nev - er end His Word de - clares__ this

*Verse 2:*

I know the journey seems so long, you feel you're walking on your own,

But there has never been a step where you've walked out all alone.

Troubled soul, don't lose your heart, 'cause joy and peace He brings;

And the beauty that's in store outweighs the hurt of life's sting.

But I hold on to this hope and the promise that He brings,

That there will be a place with no more suffering.

*(To Chorus:)*

# THIS IS AMAZING GRACE

Words and Music by Jeremy Riddle,
Phil Wickham and Joshua Neil Farro
Arranged by Carol Tornquist

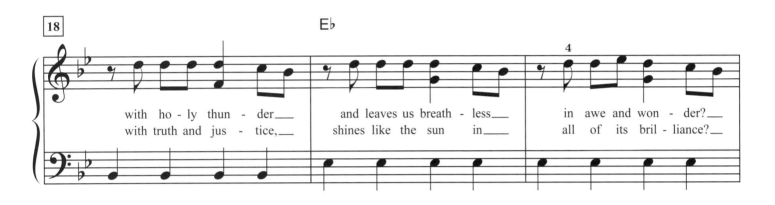

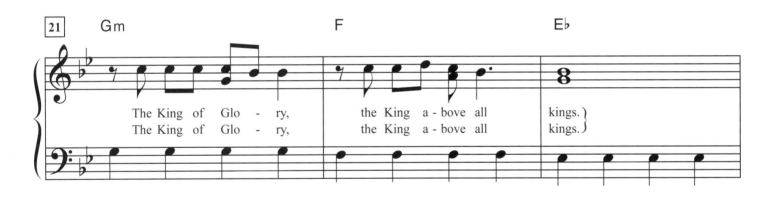

186

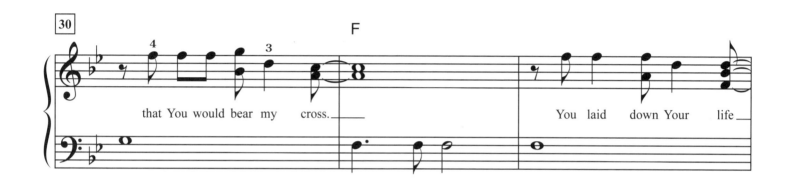

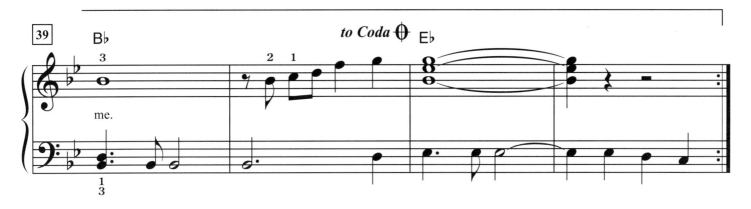

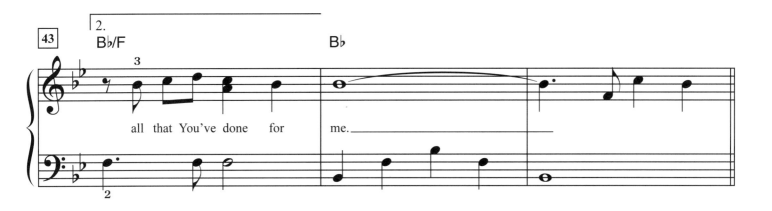

*Bridge:*

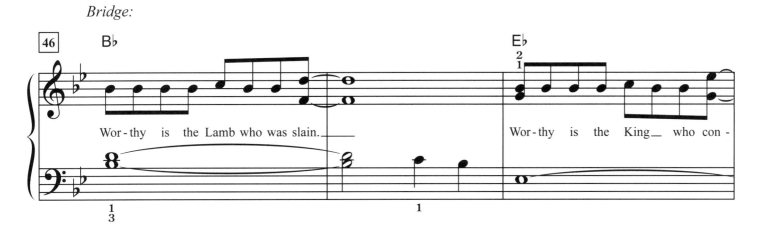

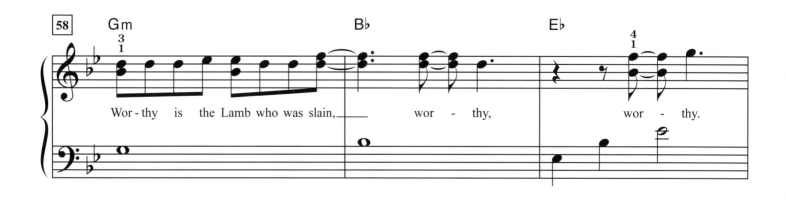

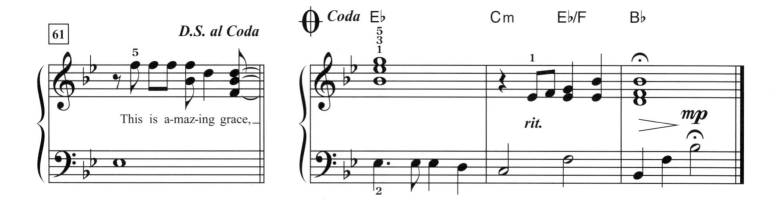

# WHO YOU ARE

Words and Music by Jason Walker,
Michael Gomez, Chad Mattson and Jon Lowry
Arranged by Carol Tornquist

*Verse 2:*
You believe in freedom, but you don't know how to choose.
You gotta step out of your feelings that you're so afraid to lose.
And ev'ry day you put your feet on the floor, you gotta walk through the door.
It's never gonna be easy, but it's all worth fighting for.
*(To Chorus:)*

# WE ARE

Words and Music by Ed Cash, Chuck Butler,
James Tealy and Hillary McBride
Arranged by Carol Tornquist

**Moderate rock, half-time feel**

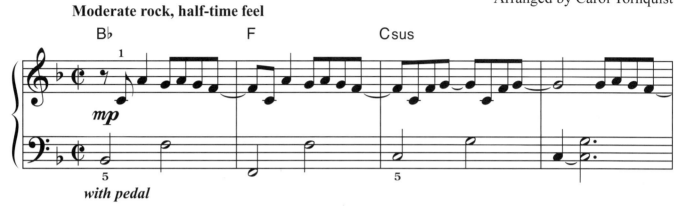

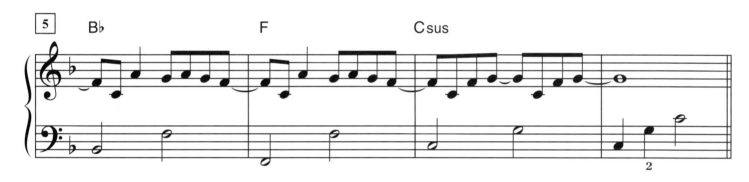

Verse:

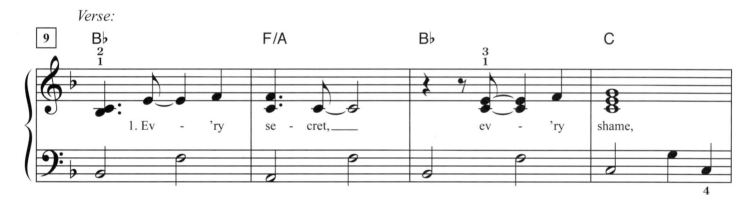

1. Ev - 'ry se - cret,___ ev - 'ry shame,

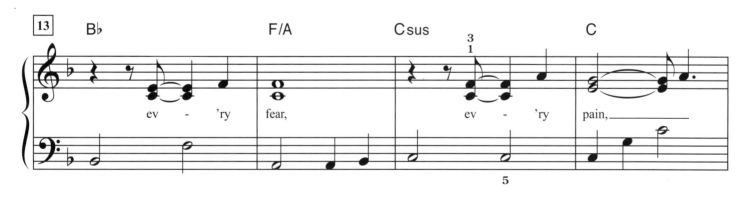

ev - 'ry fear, ev - 'ry pain,___

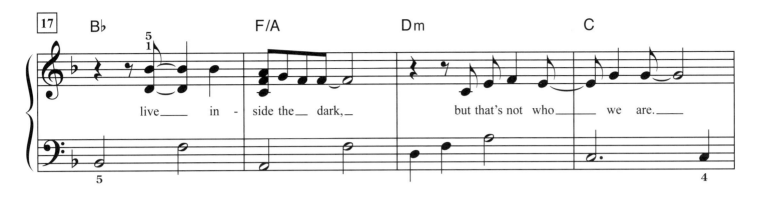

live___ in - side the__ dark,__ but that's not who__ we are.___

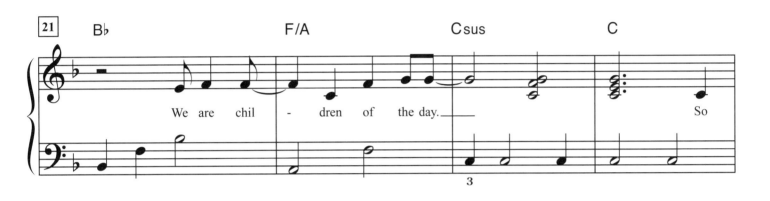

We are chil - dren of the day.___ So

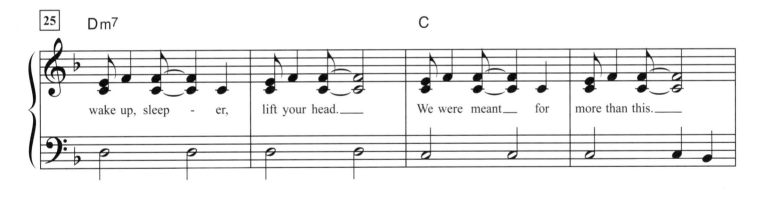

wake up, sleep - er, lift your head.___ We were meant__ for more than this.___

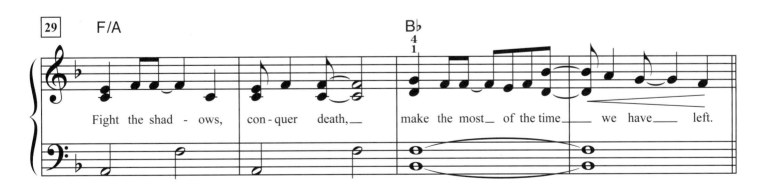

Fight the shad - ows, con - quer death,__ make the most__ of the time__ we have___ left.

𝄋 *Chorus:*

# WE BELIEVE

Words and Music by Matthew Hooper,
Richie Fike and Travis Ryan
Arranged by Carol Tornquist

Verse:

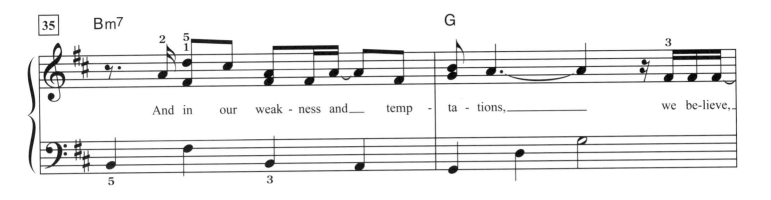

S. *Chorus:*

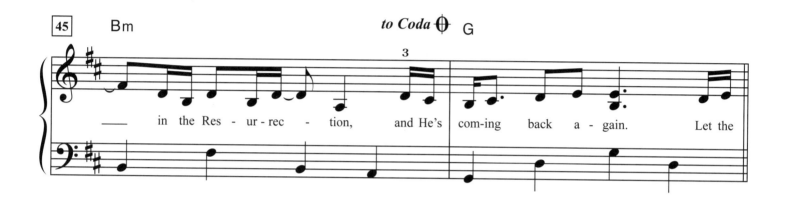

*Bridge:*

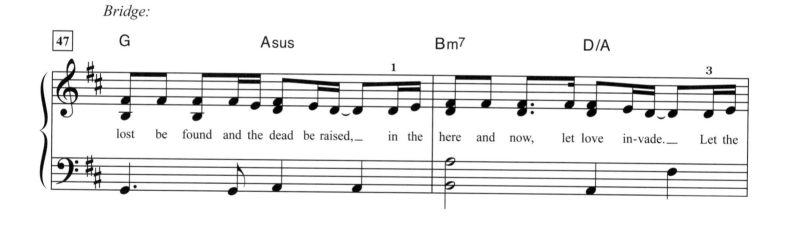

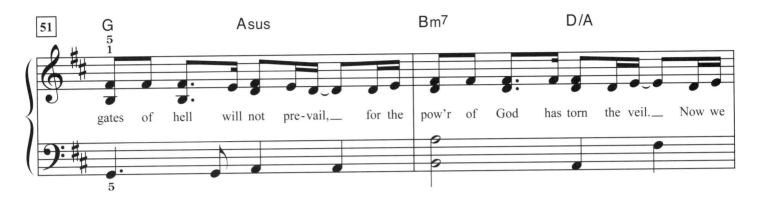

# WHO AM I

Words and Music by
Mark Hall
Arranged by Carol Tornquist

Moderate half-time feel

1. Who am I,

Verse:

_____ that the Lord of all___ the earth___ would
that the eyes that see___ my sin___ would

care to know__ my name,_____ would care to feel___ my
look on me___ with love_____ and watch me rise___ a-

hurt?_____ Who am I,_____ that the
gain?_____ Who am I,_____ that the

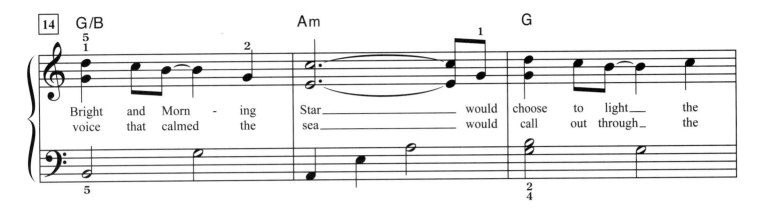

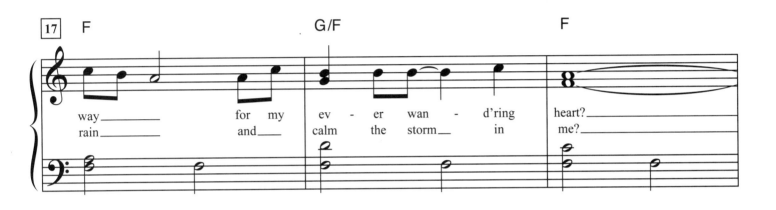

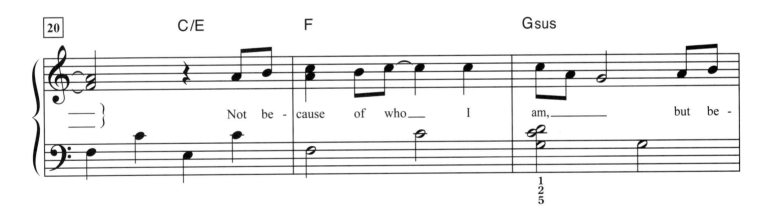

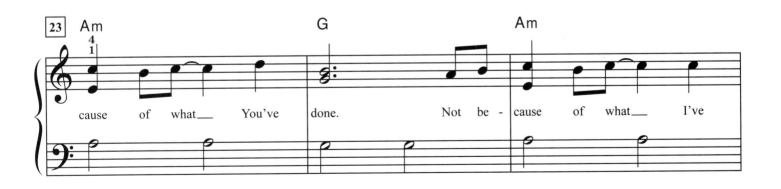

# YOU ARE

Words and Music by Rhyan Shirley,
Jared Martin, Colton Dixon and Mike Busbee
Arranged by Carol Tornquist

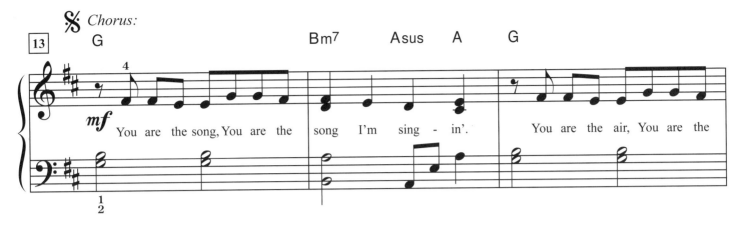

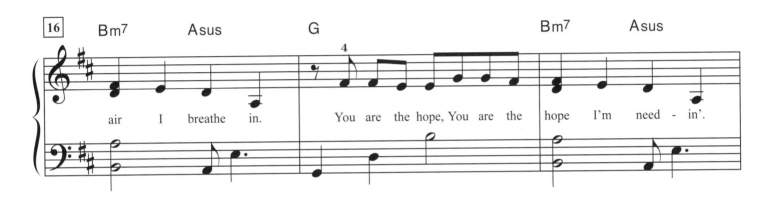

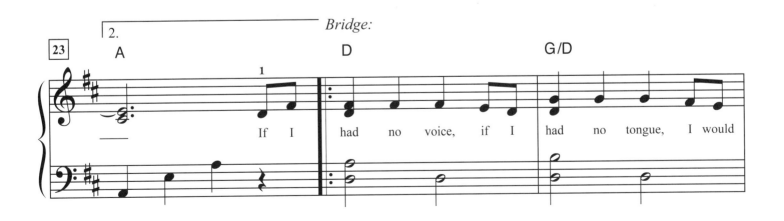

dance for You like the ris - in' sun. And when that day comes and I

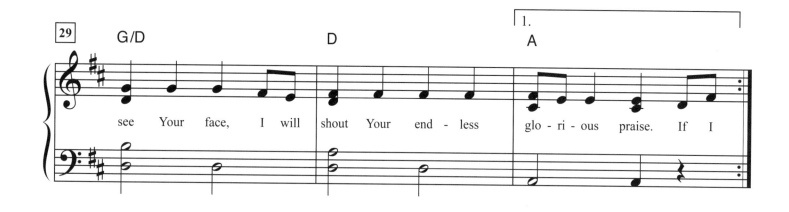

see Your face, I will shout Your end - less glo - ri - ous praise. If I

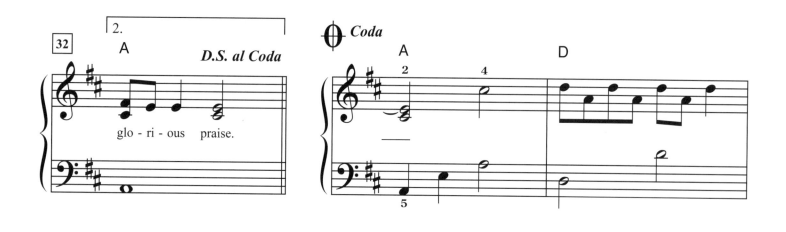

glo - ri - ous praise.

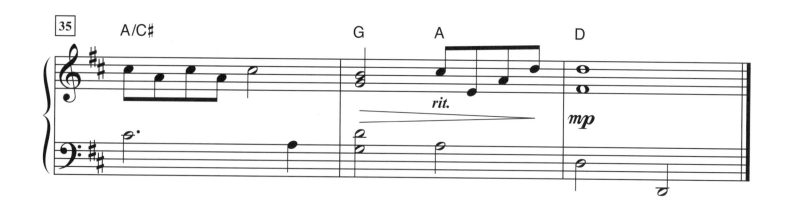

# YOUR LOVE NEVER FAILS

Words and Music by
Anthony Skinner and Chris McClarney
Arranged by Carol Tornquist

*Verse 2:*
The wind is strong and the water's deep, but I'm not alone here in these open seas,
'Cause Your love never fails.
The chasm is far too wide; I never thought I'd reach the other side.
Your love never fails, oh no, oh no.
*(To Chorus:)*

# YOUR GRACE FINDS ME

Words and Music by
Jonas Myrin and Matt Redman
Arranged by Carol Tornquist

*Coda*
*Chorus:*

There in the dark-est night of the soul, there in the sweet-est songs of

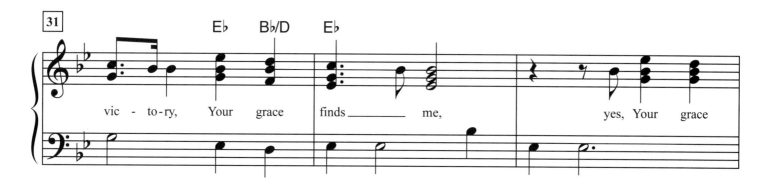

vic - to-ry, Your grace finds _____ me, yes, Your grace

finds _____ me. Your great grace, _____ oh, such

grace, _____ Your great grace, _____ oh, such grace.

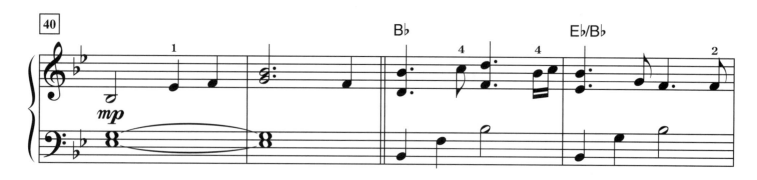

# YOUR GREAT NAME

Words and Music by
Krissy Nordhoff and Michael Neale
Arranged by Carol Tornquist

**Slowly, with expression**

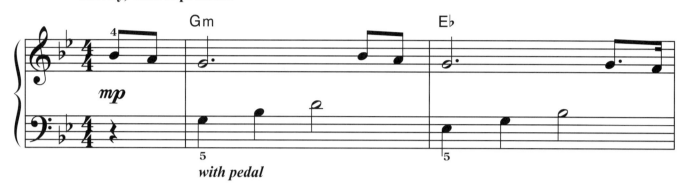

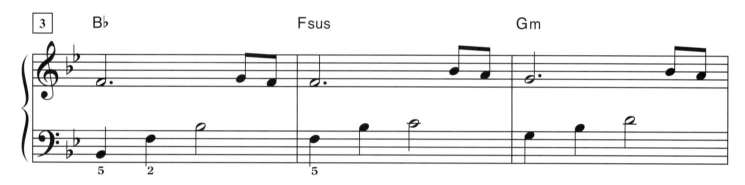

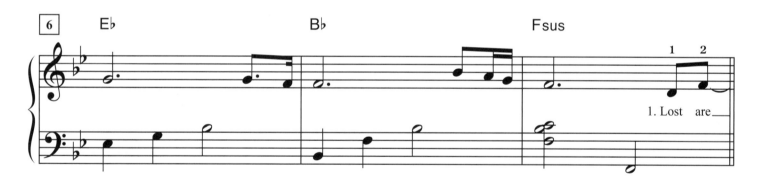

*Verse:*

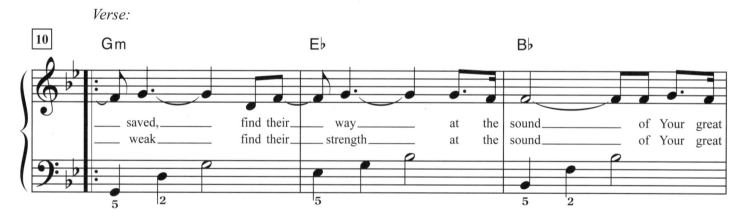

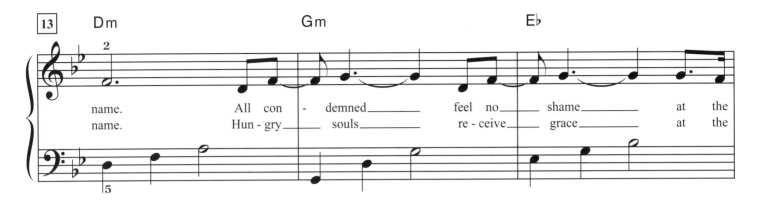

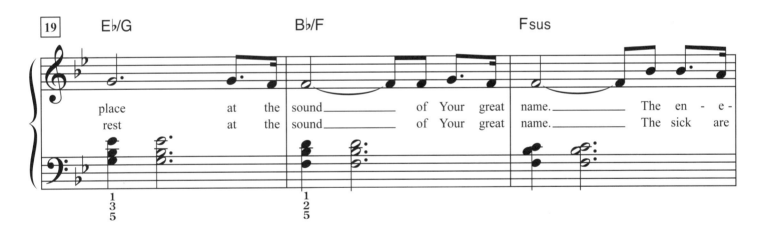

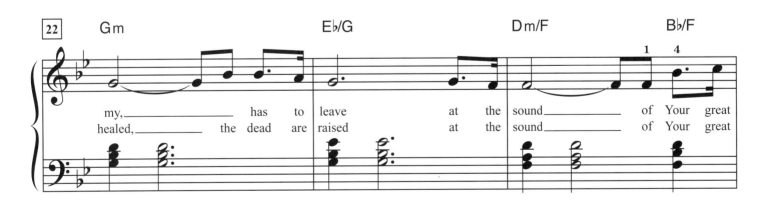

*Chorus:*

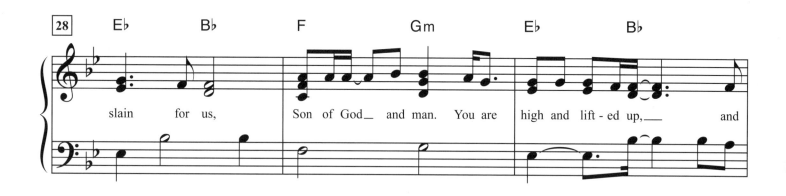

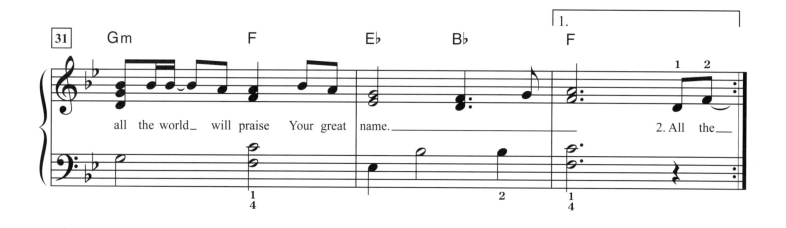

*Bridge:*

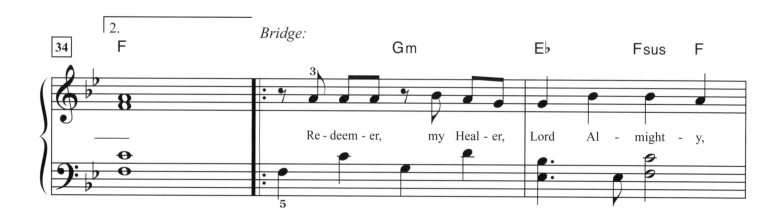

*Chorus:*

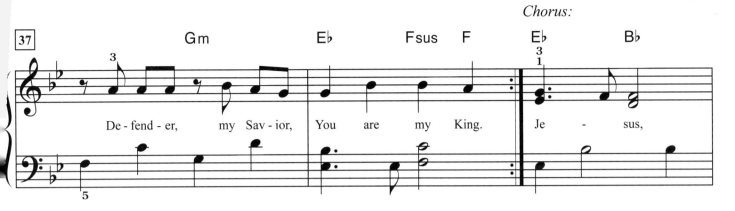

Defender, my Savior, You are my King. Jesus,

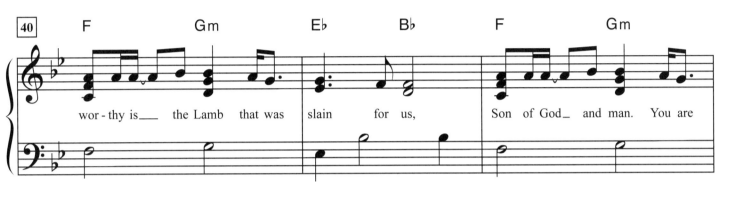

worthy is__ the Lamb that was slain for us, Son of God_ and man. You are

high and lifted up,__ and all the world_ will praise Your great name.__

Your great name.__ Your great name.

*molto rit. e dim.*  *mp*